#iPadOnly

The first real post-PC book

How to use only you iPad to work and
play…
And everything in between

Augusto Pinaud & Michael Sliwinski

To Alicia & Tomas who have a chance to understand #iPadOnly as children and most likely in a way that I am never will. To Veronica who someday will be also #iPadOnly

Augusto Pinaud

To my 4-year old daughter - Milena - the first #iPadOnly person I got to know. To my younger daughter - Emilia - who inevitably will be #iPadOnly soon. Finally, to my wife - Ewelina - the prettiest #iPadOnly geek I know :-)

Michael Sliwinski

INDEX

CHAPTER #1
INTRODUCTION

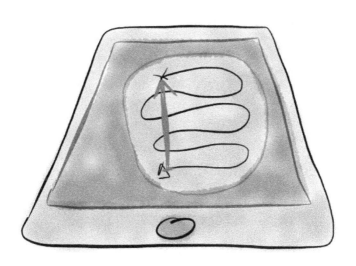

On January 27, 2010 Steve Jobs announced the iPad. He began the introduction with the following quote by the Wall Street Journal:

"Last time there was this much excitement about a tablet, it had some commandments written on it."

Everybody laughed and expected Steve to show off his new gadget right away. He kept the audience waiting and started asking them if there was room for a third category of devices, something between an iPhone and a Mac. According to Jobs for a device like that to make sense, it needed to be far better than a smartphone or a laptop at doing some key tasks. "Far better at doing some really important things", he said. Like browsing the web, processing email, enjoying and sharing photographs, watching videos, listening to music, playing games or reading eBooks.

Apple didn't stop there. They wanted the iPad to excel at many more tasks by making sure they had the software ready for this new category of devices as well. Together with the iPad, they introduced the iWork productivity suite (something similar to Microsoft Office) tailored especially for the touch screen of the iPad. Later, before the iPad shipped, they convinced the developers to build iPad-native apps - to convert their current iPhone apps and re-build them to take advantage of the bigger screen.

Going #iPadOnly

Both of us (Augusto and Michael) went #iPadOnly. Basically, this means we are now working on the iPad almost exclusively. By 'going #iPadOnly' we mean: 'performing most of our key tasks on the iPad'. Not only the tasks Steve Jobs mentioned. Practically all of them - we're working more than 80% on the iPad. We're having a blast in the process.

The first iPad began paving the #iPadOnly road. Along with the iPad 2 and an ever-increasing amount of iPad-specific apps, working via #iPadOnly all started to make sense and it's fun.

Later the same year, at the D8 Conference, Steve Jobs famously said:

"PCs are going to be like trucks"

What he meant was that the 'mainstream computing' as we know it is going to change. People will prefer to use tablets and smartphones as their 'computers' and only the skilled professionals will need 'regular PC's' for their work. Not only do we share this point of view but we also know that many more professionals than Steve envisioned can use the iPad. We know, because we work on our iPads. We manage to fit all of our work into this machine and we love every minute working on it.

Why the "#" (hash) in the name? Why "#iPadOnly" and not just "iPad only"?

Our journey started with our blog posts about our gradual shift to the iPad. We both labeled them on Twitter with an #iPadOnly hash tag - this symbolizes a new category as well as a movement. We believe more and more people will be switching to their iPads as their 'main machines' in the future. We know it's already happening. We see it happening with us and with many of our 'online friends'. That's why we believe in the #iPadOnly movement and we decided to add a '#' (hash) symbol to the book title - to manifest this new movement and paradigm shift.

When Augusto got his iPad...

It was April 2010 and he never thought it would be his main machine so soon. He was in love with his iPhone (you may call him an 'Apple' or better yet a 'Steve Jobs fan boy'). Holding the iPad in his hands, he was sure that Steve Jobs' vision was going to take us somewhere. He just wasn't expecting that it was going to be so far. Just a few months later he was performing most of his key tasks on the iPad.

When Michael got his iPad...

It was May 2010. Michael loved it as a 'media consumption' device and nothing more. However, just two years later, instead of upgrading his beloved MacBook Air, Michael decided to see if he could go #iPadOnly. He ordered the new iPad and never looked back.

We started writing about #iPadOnly on our blogs

We loved our transition to the iPad so much that we started sharing it on our blogs independently. Michael had his 'iPadOnly series' and Augusto 'How I work on my iPad' series. Once we discovered how much fun going #iPadOnly was, we wanted to share it with everyone.

Both of us are also productivity buffs. We share our passion for 'Getting Things Done' methodology (known as 'GTD') so we wanted to ensure we were working more productively on our iPads than we were on our regular computers. Suffice to say that once we got the hang of working #iPadOnly we were a lot more productive.

When Michael realized #iPadOnly was much more than he expected and that he wasn't going back to his laptop anymore, he fired an email to Augusto saying they were onto something and had to write a book together. Augusto agreed immediately.

So we wrote this book for you.

We decided to co-write this book to share our experiences working #iPadOnly. The good, the bad and the ugly. Not only has it been super fun to write, but we discovered much more in the process.

We stopped doing some things that we were doing before we began writing this book. Others we had to simplify or improve. Some of our workflows changed and some had to evolve because of this book. Writing this book together has been an opportunity to see, evaluate, re-test and acquire new assumptions on why and how this idea of #iPadOnly is really cool and necessary. It's been a great ride.

We questioned our assumptions.

All too often people fight change. They use the same tools for years without challenging themselves to try something new and re-evaluate what they are doing. 'If it ain't broke, don't fix it' they say. Maybe they are right, but maybe every once in a while we should break something or question an assumption in order to find a better and more fulfilling way to achieve the same goal.

Michael wanted a more portable machine and was sure that the MacBook Air 11' was a great device to migrate to from his MacBook Air 13'. Comparing the 10' iPad with the new 11' Air, he started questioning every aspect of his work and looking at new ways of accomplishing each task.

Augusto was always astounded by the fact that Michael was re-doing his home office every year. He thought Michael was wasting his time. He finally understood why when they began co-writing this book. By remodeling his home office Michael was forcing himself to see in minute detail what worked for him and what didn't, and more importantly, what stopped working and should be removed. Augusto, in the spirit of not wasting time and playing instead of working, was avoiding change to things that were working. Now he decided to follow Michael's lead and will schedule a regular yearly 'reevaluation' moment. For him, it's coming right after publishing this book.

Now it's time for you to remodel your work.

We believe most busy professionals, including you, can work #iPadOnly. We think you should question your old assumptions and see if you can work almost exclusively on this 'magical' device. Not just for the sake of it. Going #iPadOnly will force you to simplify your work, make it more rewarding, and in return, more fun. It's a new paradigm shift and it's simply amazing. This book will serve as your blueprint. In the coming chapters we'll show you what our #iPadOnly transition looked like, what we changed and what we tweaked. We'll also demonstrate which apps, services and accessories we used that facilitated our transition to the #iPadOnly world. Hold tight - it's going to be a great ride.

CHAPTER #2
COMPUTING BECOMES MUCH MORE INTIMATE

"People laugh at me because I describe the iPad as magical. You have a much more direct and intimate relationship with the Internet and media and apps and your content."
- Steve Jobs, D8 Conference

Humans not only need intimate social relationships, they also need and love to touch other people... and things. Once you started using your iPad for some time, think about the last time you touched the screen of your laptop trying to mimic what you can do on the iPad. We have all done it! Touching the screen directly is better than just looking and clicking with the mouse. The iPad is all about touching.

Before the iPad there was Microsoft with the Tablet PC concept - an expensive technology that created the first laptops that allowed you to interact with the screen. Many of the people that had them loved them. There was something about the interaction with the screen that a regular PC could not replicate, even though it required the use of an annoying stylus. It was so much fun to 'touch the screen' directly and watch the computer react to your touch.

We both had TabletPCs before we switched to the Mac. We missed 'the touch' of our old PCs but we liked the new Mac OSX platform. Our 'touchy' feeling came back even stronger when we started working on the iPad. Steve Jobs was right; the finger is the best stylus ever. We could really touch our email! We could touch the articles, swipe them, and rotate images. We could actually create a closer and more intimate relationship not only with the device, but with the content. It felt like we really were connected to the contents of the screen more than when using a laptop or even the TabletPC.

In addition, the developers have been bringing innovative approaches to their iPad apps that encourage you to use your fingers and play with the content. It's fun, more intuitive and has a more natural feel.

That's why we agree with Steve Jobs - it really is a more intimate way of computing and after more than a year of working almost exclusively on the iPad, we can't say we're tired of it. Lots of apps are being designed in a way to help you use gestures, swipe, touch and pinch and simply touch the screen even more. The fun has only just begun and there is no turning back. This new and intimate way of interacting with our computers and content is here to stay.

Going #iPadOnly is a personal Journey.

Most people are convinced that the iPad can only be used for 'media consumption'. They miss the opportunity to change the paradigms that have them tied to their laptops.

In the early 90's, when the first laptops began to appear, many people didn't believe that they would ever be as powerful as desktops. The rest is history.

In 2010 when the iPad was announced people didn't believe that it would be powerful enough to replace and improve modern computing. History likes to repeat itself. Previously laptops were considered 'underpowered' and for several years now people have been choosing them instead of the big desktop computers. Today tablets like the iPad are in more households than ever before and people are discovering that they can do much more with them.

We see people discovering that their iPad can be so much more than just a companion device. People are beginning to wonder if they can, like us, go #iPadOnly. On the other hand, they keep telling us that 'this or that can't be done on the iPad'. We discovered that almost every job can be done on the iPad, but perhaps a bit differently than on a regular PC.

This book was written using only our iPads. Augusto has written more than eight books on his iPad. He has also used his iPad to help manage sales in the US, Canada and Latin America. He consulted and helped companies change their sales, and provided marketing and product development to generate growth - again using only his iPad. Augusto jumped to his iPad looking for a more dynamic portable work environment, and quickly discovered that he could do so much on this new platform.

Michael is writing, coding and managing as the CEO of Nozbe. He also, is only using his iPad. When Michael wanted to simplify his setup and become more mobile he switched to the iPad. As a productivity guy, he was curious to learn if the app-revolution and post-PC era were really true. Via #iPadOnly, he's busy running a very successful time and project management application (with a team of 15 people), he's the editor of the *Productive! Magazine* and he's a blogger.

We're not alone nor are we that special. Like Augusto and Michael, many people are using their iPads as their main machines. Many stopped using their old laptops and desktops and are changing how they do things. What you will find here is not just one way, but two examples of how to use your iPad as the main machine. We share a passion for productivity but we do different things for a living and we each approached the #iPadOnly process in our own way.

Getting to #iPadOnly is a personal journey. You might start with only a fraction of the time working on the iPad but gradually you'll see how this will change and you'll start loving your iPad not just for 'consuming content' but also for creating it. We hope you will find many ideas in this book and it will guide you through your own #iPadOnly journey.

www.youtube.com/iPadOnlyBook
Video #1: The Office Evolution with the iPad in mind.

iPad is not a PC. It's so much more.

In Augusto's opinion the hardest challenge to work #iPadOnly is to be open to rebuilding your old habits and workflows. Michael shares Augusto's view, highlighting that many people want to configure the iPad the same way as they did their PC or Mac. At first iPad seems like a very limited computing experience, but later these limitations come as blessings in disguise. They force us to re-examine our way of operating and to totally rebuild our workflows, and most of all – to simplify and improve them.

The problem with workflows and habits is that they quickly become invisible; you simply don't notice that they even exist. Confronting them and being willing to change them might be one of the hardest challenges you will find on the journey to #iPadOnly. In our experience most of those changes create an improvement on the conditions that existed before. But even on those rare occasions in which they don't, simply becoming conscious of a habit or a workflow is worth the exercise.

The most interesting and unexpected thing while we wrote this book was the fact that the workflows that we believed to be solid and set, have been evaluated and reconsidered. We have learned new things from one other, evolved in the use of our machines, and without a doubt convinced ourselves even more that #iPadOnly is the way!

The "because you can" problem.

Working on the iPad can be very tricky. It does many things better than a smartphone or a laptop, but it is not a replacement for either of them. It is not that the machine isn't capable or powerful enough, it is just because it's different.

The biggest obstacle when people want to go #iPadOnly is usually themselves. We forget that this is a device of that third category. We have our habits ingrained so deeply that we try to bring them to use on this device in the same way we use them in our 'computer life'. We want the iPad to function in 'the same way the PC does, just better'. It doesn't work like that.

The iPad was never designed to substitute the computer in a literal sense. It was designed to help us realize we didn't need a full-blown computer for most of our computing tasks. In order to accomplish that, you, the user, needs to be willing to change some of those old 'PC' habits. Many things will come naturally to you and will make sense. Other things are not going to work for your specific circumstances and will have to be re-evaluated.

Because you can.

In terms of horsepower, the iPad is not as powerful as a modern laptop computer. But then again, it doesn't have to be. The computers we work on these days are too powerful for our needs and because they are so powerful, we mismanage and try to do too many things on them. Things we'd otherwise delegate to some apps or services. The traditional computer is very powerful and the apps you have are very powerful, too. Too many options, lots of bells and whistles (just open Microsoft Word and see for yourself). All this creates an abundance of possibilities that gives us a perfect argument not to do our work but start 'playing with our work' and 'tweaking our work' and doing 'lots of administrative tasks'. Why? Because we feel the need to use and maximize this powerful computer with its powerful applications. In simple terms, 'just because we can'.

Things are different on the iPad. Over here you've got a not-so-powerful computer but powerful enough to run its operating system and apps. The apps seem less powerful, but they are more focused. Open Apple Pages on the iPad and on the Mac. It's more-or-less the same app. Thanks to the iCloud you can work on the same documents on both devices. But on the iPad, it's more focused. It's simpler to use and that's what helps you focus on your work.

Working with more focus is a different experience to what most people using powerful machines are used to doing. You discover that the old ways of doing things are not working on your iPad and you suddenly have to 'design new workflows'. You have to redefine how to process emails, write blog posts, review spreadsheets, send feedback to your team and much more. It gives you an opportunity to take a fresh look at all of this, evaluate many processes and move forward with improved efficiency. Here are some of our examples

Michael and the "Downloads" folder problem:

"When I received an email with an invoice attached on the Mac, I'd download the attachment to my Downloads folder. Later that week I'd go though of all of my 'Downloads' and move some of them to my Dropbox or Evernote. Not that big of a deal, but if you've got hundreds of attachments to go through every week, it's no fun at all. Not only that, it may be really time consuming, but because it works you may have not looked into the process in detail to find a better way.

When I started working on the iPad I realized that the Evernote app gives me a unique email address for forwarding my emails. The forwarded emails are added to Evernote automatically. This option was available before the iPad came about. I knew that, but never gave it much thought because I didn't have to. Because I *could* save the attachment and process it later, I did just that. On the iPad a 'Downloads' folder doesn't exist. There isn't a place to store these documents for processing again at the end of the week. I said again, because at the end of the week I needed to revisit this folder and make another decision. After I added my unique Evernote email address to my contacts and changed my own workflow for how I process invoices, my workflow has been streamlined to this. Receive invoice. Forward to Evernote. One click, one action, done. I soon realized many other apps offer the same 'email gateways'. I now send files to Dropbox, tasks to Nozbe, and much more. It is a different workflow - no more saving, processing, or organizing later - fewer steps, more time saved. Working on the iPad made me catch my inefficiency and re-think the process. Thanks to these little changes and by modifying and adjusting workflows, I can get to 'inbox zero' on my iPad much faster."

Augusto and his tax receipts:

"Before my 2011 tax declarations, I used to stack hardcopy folders on top of the file cabinet with all my receipts and any relevant information. I would drive to my accountant's office with a huge pile of papers and folders for her to process. In 2012, I began sending anything that I believed to be relevant for taxes to Evernote. I scan (using the iPad camera) any receipt that wasn't already in digital format. When tax time came, I simply opened Evernote and forwarded everything in the folder to my accountant. She was thrilled. I used to spend a lot of time reorganizing the hardcopy file. Regardless how organized the folders were, I needed to be sure I sent everything to her. Now, I don't need to think or remember anything; I simply forward the content of the Evernote folder to the accountant, and it's done! The previous system worked, but this idea appeared when I began looking for a way to be #iPadOnly. If I need to find the original receipts, I can. That part of the process is just as painful as it has always been!"

Mail attachments and the iPad paradigm shift.

How many times have you received an email from someone telling you to look at an attached document, only to find they forgot to attach anything to the message? You'd have to reply to remind them. And only then they'd send you yet another email with the attachment. That's because on a traditional computer you write the email message first and then attach your document.

The iPad works differently. First, you open an app like Photos, Evernote, Dropbox or any other app that contains content you want to send. Next, you tap the 'Share' button and compose the email message with the attachment already in place. You begin with the 'attachment' and later write your email. Sounds trivial, but it's an entire paradigm shift.

Going #iPadOnly changes everything.

It is examples like these that give us the opportunity to see, evaluate, re-test and acquire new assumptions on why and how this idea of #iPadOnly is both fun and more efficient. The irony is that it's the constraints of the iOS that make our processes highly effective and efficient. Developers of the iPad apps are learning more and more about this 'magical' device. Their focus is on reducing steps and finding innovative solutions that aren't possible in a traditional computing environment.

www.youtube.com/iPadOnlyBook

Video #2: iPad is powerful enough - your PC/Mac is too powerful.

There are more tricks like that and we'll discuss them in this book. The thing is, with the powerful computer we're lazy and we do stuff we shouldn't do *just because we can!* On the iPad, you have to carefully think about these things, but when you do, you discover that many workflows, processes and things we do in our daily life can be simplified and improved. As a result you enjoy working on the iPad a lot more. We know we do and after you read this book and work on your own workflows, you will too.

In the future chapters of this book we'll show you how we:

* write and publish blog posts
* write and publish books
* manage our businesses
* manage photos and share them with family
* edit and share videos
* write code and code revision
* process consistent feedback loops with our co-workers
* deal with email
* read
* listen
* and everything else... in an #iPadOnly fashion.

Our life before the iPad

After reading this book, you'll find our computer setups were not always as lean and simple as they seemed. There was a time that we both had a complicated system with many parts and heavy equipment. Let's look into what that was like so you can understand and appreciate a little more about why we are so happy to be where we are now.

It took us a while to get to #iPadOnly but it was well worth it.

www.youtube.com/iPadOnlyBook
Video #3: What's impossible to do on the iPad?

Before Michael went #iPadOnly...

To understand why I choose to go #iPadOnly, let's quickly go through the history of my computing life. I've been using computers for a long, long time. I started as a 10-year old with an IBM PC XT when everyone else was playing games on their Commodore c64 or Amiga 500. As time evolved, I kept improving my computer setup. I went from XT to AT 286 later to 386, 486, Pentium, etc.

In the summer of 2000, I got my first laptop computer; a Compaq Armada with a Pentium II processor. It was the heaviest laptop I ever had. It weighed a whopping 6 lbs. (3 kg) and had an astonishing 2 hours of battery life. I loved that machine and used it for two years while I was in college. Carrying it to school every day put a toll on my back. I knew I needed something lighter.

I often experimented with different laptops, always trying to find the lightest possible model. When people would ask me about the most important feature in a laptop computer, I'd always say 'weight' and 'battery life.' They looked at me like I was crazy. They expected some spec like RAM, hard drive capacity or stuff like that from someone that really understands computers. To me, that was secondary. I cared about the looks of the machine, the weight and size more than anything else.

At some point I bought a Fujitsu P1200 laptop with a touch-display. It was a novelty on many levels. I loved the small size (1kg) and a screen I could touch. The problem was, it was a slow computer. I moved on and discovered a new 'breed' of computers called TabletPCs and bought the best there was at the time - a Toshiba M200. I used that device for many years. The TabletPC concept seemed very cool at first. I loved that the screen turned and you could write on it using the Wacom digitizer. It was a fun machine and a complete showoff - people would always ask me how that 'tablet thing' really worked. This laptop was heavy though (2kg ~ 4 lbs), and the TabletPC Windows version wasn't all that useful in the day-to-day work after the initial 'wow' factor wore off.

In 2008, Steve Jobs unveiled the MacBook Air and it was the first laptop I really fell in love with. Seriously, it was love at first sight. It was light, sexy, curvy, and fast. It was a stunner. Being a PC guy, I didn't want to ditch the Windows platform. But after a year, I finally gave up and bought a MacBook Air. This was a major change for me even though it met what I considered the two most important features on a machine, weight and battery life. The switch from the Windows platform to the Mac was painful on one hand and rewarding on the other. It made me rethink everything I knew about my computing life. How to store files, how to use email, how to use the all new apps that were native on the Mac. It took me a few good months to get there but I finally did. I loved the outcome! I worked better, I was more productive and I worked on a very sexy machine with a very nice operating system.

When the first iPad appeared on the market, I quickly bought one of those too (I already had the iPhone). Again, I appreciated the same elegance of the iOS and Mac OSX. However, to me the iPad was a cool gadget, a nice thing to have and a great media consumption device. I was reading ebooks, RSS feeds, watching YouTube. At that point it was simply a consumption device. All that changed around 2012 when the iPad 3 with Retina screen appeared on the market. I decided to buy the cellular version to see if I could squeeze more use out of it. It was also the moment when I was contemplating buying a smaller MacBook Air - the 11 inch version to replace my trusty 13 inch model.

Then it struck me - why not use the iPad instead of the MacBook Air? I decided the iOS platform was mature enough to give it a serious try. I thought about it one more time and it met my important criteria for computers. The weight was less than half a kilogram (providing total portability), and it had a 10 hour battery. I also found other attractive features like:

- Optional keyboard
- Ability to work horizontally or vertically
- Real 'instant-on'
- A variety of fantastic apps

Pretty strong arguments, right? On top of that, an opportunity to rethink my computing paradigms, once again, to determine if I could learn something new.

So I jumped in.".

Before Augusto went #iPadOnly.

It was 1985. My first computer was a Macintosh. The entire operating system, applications and files lived on floppy disks that had a whooping 400KB. It came with Mac Write and Mac Paint as part of the software. Our household has not been without a computer since. A series of Mac and Desktop PCs came and went. In 1995 I bought an Apple PowerBook 140. After that, I never wanted a desktop again. I loved the portability of the laptop, even if the battery didn't last very long. I loved the fact that I could be super portable.

I have always liked the idea that technology allowed us to work from anywhere and there is no need to be in a physical location. I have never been a huge fan of offices.

The problem was that in order to accomplish everything that I had to do, I needed to carry an incredible amount of technology with me. At the peak of this I had a Tablet PC, a Mac, a PC Laptop (mind you, that I once sold software and then accessories for the PC) scanner, printer, files, and much more. My bag was massive and weighed over 40 lbs. (18 kilos). As I was writing this, I laughed because on a bad day now, my bag is a little over 4lbs (1.8 Kilos) and its contents are much more powerful than the previous 40lbs of equipment.

It is the simplification to my computer mess that is one of the things I really love and enjoy about the iPad. I have a better set of tools, more power, more capabilities and it's less expensive.

I have taken this opportunity to revise, change, evolve and in some instances eliminate some of the workflows from the TabletPC and Mac days. There are many things that I would not like to go back to, ever again.

There is something that really changed with this setup that I really love and enjoy. It's quite simple. Between the iPad and the iPhone, I need less and less. In addition, every time I consider it is time to upgrade, I now consider another iPad, not another MacBook.

I know that someday I may replace that old MacBook for another, but not until certain things in my workflow cannot be done on the iPad. At this time, I believe that the iOS platform is mature enough to allow you to totally work from it. There are things that the iPad brings to the table that a combination of Mac and PC never will. It is not only a simplification factor (and trust me, I have no desire to drag around an additional 36lbs of equipment) but true portability, an amazing battery life and the ability to work intimately with your machine. I jumped onto this in 2011 and I have never looked back.".

iPad's KISS - Keep It Simple, Stupid!

When we switched to #iPadOnly, one of the most annoying things was the fact that we had to redesign all of our workflows from scratch. It was also the most liberating thing - we could take our time, find the appropriate apps and finally revise everything we were doing on the computer and make it 'leaner' and 'more focused'.

The iPad also drove us to take the plunge and move to the cloud. Most of the things we use are now in the cloud. Michael keeps his files in Dropbox, his notes in Evernote, tasks in Nozbe and settings in the iCloud. Augusto also has his documents in Dropbox, his file cabinet in Evernote, his notes in the Notepad application synced with iCloud and his tasks and GTD system in Omnifocus. Everything has its place.

This 'living in the cloud' allowed us to simplify the process of sharing. Because we use the cloud, sharing of files, ideas and notes became easy. As we mentioned earlier, before the iPad, in order to share we'd first need to fire up the email client, write an email and later start searching for the attachments to add to that email. Many times over, we simply forgot about attaching the file and would have to send the recipient another message with the attachment and an apology.

On the iPad you simply go to Dropbox, Evernote, Photos or the app needed. Choose files, notes or images you want to share, choose 'email', and send. The iPad simply reverses the process providing these three benefits:

* We never forget attachments, because we start with them.
* Because we don't start in the email program, there is no temptation to read other email messages and get distracted

from our current work

* When we have 'large files' to send, we send links to them, instead of attaching the file - as the files are in the cloud, people can access them through the links we send. No more sending of heavy emails!

Not everything is perfect, and there are things that still annoy us with some cloud apps. Both Dropbox and Evernote apps have seen some improvements, but Dropbox doesn't 'sync' folders on the iPad so we cannot have an entire folder 'offline' on our iPads... and with 64GB iPads we'd have plenty of space for our files. Evernote does sync notebooks offline (if you have a Premium account) but over there the 'note processing' is very tiresome. To move a note from one notebook to another takes quite a few taps. Other than that, we love these apps.

One of the most important things for Augusto is the fact that his iPad offers him the ability to simplify the writing process. We both write in Byword where everything we write is saved automatically to Dropbox. When Michael needs a 'rich-formatted' text with bold and italics, he writes in Markdown - where he can preview his text files and blog posts directly from the app and copy the resulting formatted text any way he chooses. Since we began writing this book Augusto has been experimenting with Markdown but it is not yet something that comes naturally to him.

It is the use of this simple writing app that helps us focus on writing and (again) makes sharing our writing a breeze and gives us peace of mind, knowing everything we write is automatically saved on the iPad and in Dropbox.

Over the course of writing this book we experimented with different apps and ways of sharing text. We eventually ditched Google Drive and Google Docs (too clunky and complicated on the iPad) and wrote everything in Byword by sharing an

#iPadOnly folder in Dropbox. Michael also ditched his
Nebulous Notes and AI Writer apps in favor of Byword and
he's happy with his choice.

Our bags are getting smaller and smaller but also more
powerful as they shrink. If you carry the iPad you can scan, fax,
access reference files, sign documents, create documents, write,
edit, exchange information or simply have a FaceTime or
Skype call. All of that capability comes without additional
weight. In many ways the simplification of the office
equipment you need is amazing.

It is this ability to work in the Cloud, with more focus, with
simple yet more powerful tools on the iPad that allow you to
truly streamline your work. There are a lot more simplifications
on the iPad but these stand out at first. We'll talk about more
of them in the next chapters of the book.

Hold on tight and you'll discover why going #iPadOnly is not
as crazy of an idea as you might think. You may discover that it
brings back the focus and simplification to your work thanks
to the iPad's unique software, hardware design and capabilities.

www.youtube.com/iPadOnlyBook
Video #4: Simplification and Minimalism on the iPad.

Why moving to the "cloud" is important.

Moving completely "to the cloud" was something Michael
Moving completely 'to the cloud' was something Michael
always wanted to do but never got around to completely doing.
With the iPad he had no choice. Even though he owns a 64GB
iPad, its storage capacity still pales with the comparison of his
home office Mac Mini with 1TB disk and Time Capsule with
2TB.

Augusto wasn't as eager to jump to the cloud as Michael. He
was always on the go and didn't want to depend on an Internet
connection in hotels or slow cellular connections of his phone.
As he was trying to simplify his setup and reducing the weight
of that bag, he understood that the cloud may provide a good
solution, so he finally jumped in with both feet.

We believe there are three main reasons to have your data in
the cloud - convenience, simplicity and security.

Convenience of the Cloud

Having your data in the cloud means it is stored on a remote
server infrastructure. Basically, this means you can access it
from anywhere in the world, with any device you want. It
works like magic. You can use an iPad, iPhone or any Mac or
PC to access this data. You no longer have to worry about
'some file I created once' because the file is always there, in the
cloud, within your reach from anywhere you're located. With
any device. Including your beloved iPad. That also means, if
you need to restore your data on the go, all you need is a
device and the connection to your data.

Simplification of the Cloud

The process of going to the cloud is like moving to a new home - you have to go through most of your stuff before you put it in the boxes to move to a new place. This means you get to decide if you still need this or that. You will discover there are a lot of things that are not only unnecessary but irrelevant when you really stop to consider them. First you need to decide which 'clouds' (i.e. 'cloud services') you want to use - and we'll talk about this in just a bit. Second, you have to move your data to the cloud. Our goal was to be able to access everything we needed from the iPad. Michael deleted 60% of the 'stuff' he had on his computer in the process - files he'd never need or that were no longer relevant to anything he did; Augusto went from a set of 500GB hard drives (one for the PC, one for backup on the go, one for backup at home) to less than 10GB of space. Setting up the 'cloud services' right, we finally knew exactly which piece of information belonged where. Going #iPadOnly made us go 'cloud only' and simplified our entire computer setup even more than we'd anticipated.

Security in the Cloud

Putting your data in the cloud may seem scary for many of you. Michael was more confident about it as he runs a cloud service of sorts himself (Nozbe). He knows how much companies invest in making the infrastructure reliable and safe. How many backups, and backups of backups are actually being performed. Michael knows there's virtually no way for cloud companies to lose any piece of user data as they have it backed up and duplicated safely in several places in real time. All of the cloud services work like this - they live and breathe with data safety in mind because the users must trust their cloud providers. If the trust is gone, the cloud business is gone. This was Augusto's biggest concern, mostly because of lack of knowledge, but after he spent some time listening and learning he understood that the cloud was safer than his current setup of carrying everything on external and internal hard drives

www.youtube.com/iPadOnlyBook
Video #5: Why the Cloud is so important for the iPad.

Cloud is where it's at.

Now that we've moved entirely to the cloud and we've been working like this for more than a year, we can't imagine working the way we did before we moved to the cloud. Thanks to having our data in the cloud, we know where our data is, we can access it from anywhere we want and we feel confident that our data is stored in a safe place at all times.

Without a doubt Dropbox played a big role in making the cloud stronger. It was the first service to make the syncing of data files almost invisible, ubiquitous, and accessible to anyone. These days we have a lot of data in the cloud. The iCloud is handling contacts, calendars, and photos and Dropbox is handling our files. You start worrying less and less about backups and more and more about dependency.

On the other hand, as the iPad has significant storage, most of the things we use every day are synced with the iPad and we can access them offline - without an Internet connection. Contrary to the 'Chromebooks' idea and other online-only devices, the iPad works great without an Internet connection and you're confident the changes you make will be synced later.

If Dropbox disappears today it will be something really painful that will disturb cloud life significantly. On the other hand, it is these cloud services that allow us to simplify many things. It allowed us to focus on the work and not on how to reach the different devices and applications. This book it is an example of it. We can start to write this document on the iPhone, continue on the iPad, back to the iPhone and finally, thanks to the cloud, when the time is right to share it or send it to the editor, the cloud will have the last version of the document, like magic. Michael has worked on the book from Spain, Poland and the Netherlands. Augusto has worked from multiple cities in the US. All transparent, all invisible, all 'in the cloud'.

Multi-tasking or multi-distracting?

When people learn that we work #iPadOnly they ask us about multitasking and complain about iPad's lack of having 'windows' with different apps all over its tiny 10-inch screen (or the even the smaller 7 inch screen on the iPad mini). We are simply embracing the constraints of the iPad. We believe these constraints are blessings in disguise.

We don't multi-task. Most of the time, the only thing that comes out of multi-tasking is that you are multi-distracting yourself. People really can't do several things at once. We think we can but it's not what is really happening. We can quickly switch our focus from one task to another and it gives an impression of multi-tasking but in reality it is single-tasking with a switch. Women are better at this than men (at least our wives are better than us) because of their nature - they are designed to be able to take care of the child, while cooking a dinner, while reading a book and working. Again, this is just a focus switch. Not a real multi-tasking ability.

When we multi-task, what happens is that with each switch of focus we need to get accustomed to the new task - and it takes a little bit of time. Studies have long shown that people who multi-task don't really work faster. They think they do, but they'd actually be better off doing the same things one after another - not alongside one another. This is why iPad's constraint of 'one app at the time' is so great.

Here's what Augusto writes about his single-tasking experience:

"As I'm typing this on my iPad there is nothing to distract me. My email client, my Twitter client, and my other apps, are all in the background. All I see now is a black screen with white fonts. No menus, options, or anything else- just the text I'm typing. The only option I have is to write or not to write. It's binary. It's easy. It's focused. And it works."

Single-tasking is good for you. Ask any productivity expert. We have been using GTD (Getting Things Done) methodology in our daily lives for the last decade and we've studied all the other productivity methodologies and techniques out there. We feel more productive and are getting more done by being single-taskers. We believe that multitasking is ineffective and because of that we try to avoid it as much as we can.

It is not that we have always been averse to multitasking; we have had multiple computers working at the same time over the years, two or more monitors and more. This is something that the iPad brought back to us. For many it is something that the iPad failed at, the lack of multitasking. For us, it is one of our favorite features; the ability to use one and only one application at a time. As we write text on the iPad, no email is being sent out or received, no tweet is being written, there is no weather or stock market distraction. It's our text and us.

The COMMAN+TAB problem.

For many people working on computers today, the biggest enemy regarding their own productivity is the infamous app switcher: COMMAND+TAB (or CONTROL+TAB on Windows). To switch to a different application on the iPad you have to either double click on the home button and choose another app, or use a four-finger gesture. It's pretty easy but takes a little longer than switching between apps with COMMAND+TAB on the Mac, thus making the process more conscious and less automatic on the iPad. We get into a hypnotic state in front of our computers. The reason you open the browser to research something for work and end up in Facebook is not because you aren't busy or because you don't know that you will be wasting time. It is because you can make the switch so quick and basically with zero effort. That is why you don't break the hypnotic state. We can change everything without taking our hands off the keyboard. We can open the browser and open something, create a second tab and open something else. When we are in that hypnotic state, that ability to open one thing after another always plays against us. That is the reason Augusto recommends using different browsers for work and play.

The iPad brings at least two incredible benefits to help you fight the multi-distraction battle.:

First - one app at the time. This helps you get focused on your work, not on your machine.

Second - the apps as such are more focused.

They have fewer features, less cluttered menus, less options - their authors and developers chose the most important features. That's why you will find people often prefer the iPad apps to their Mac counterparts.

www.youtube.com/iPadOnlyBook

Video #6: Single Tasking on the iPad - one app at a time for max focus.

How about the iPad mini?

We started working #iPadOnly before the iPad mini was introduced. Now that half a year has passed since the iPad mini introduction, people constantly ask us whether they should choose the 'big' iPad or the 'mini'. In Michael's household there are two iPads - the big one (Michael's) and the mini (Michael's wife). In Augusto's case there were two big ones, but in the process of writing this book he now has 1 big and 2 minis. (It is actually Michael's fault that the iPad situation changed in Augusto's household).

Michael bought the iPad mini just to test the Nozbe's iPad application on the smaller screen. When his wife saw the mini, she took it and asked Michael to configure it for her. She downloaded her favorite apps and completely ditched her touch-capable Kindle. Then, she asked for a pretty red cover. She loves the mini! It travels with her to the same places her Kindle traveled. It fits in most of her purses and she literally takes it everywhere she goes. She uses the Kindle app, plays Solitaire, checks email, browses the web... and does everything she was able to do on the regular iPad..

After Augusto's wife heard that story, the first iPad mini arrived at their home to replace her trusty iPad 2. Augusto wanted to see if an iPad mini could replace his big one but his wife wouldn't give it back to him so he decided to get a mini for himself... and at the end of the chapter you'll learn what he thinks about it.

Where iPad Mini wins... According to Michael

"The iPad mini has a cool form-factor and is a bit differently designed than its big brother. It weighs half of what the big one weighs and is significantly smaller (close to 8 inch vs. more than 10 inches). Because it's so much lighter and just a little smaller, it's definitely more portable than the big one. It still doesn't fit the usual men's jacket pocket but its size resembles that of a traditional book. This is why my wife loves her mini so much. She loves the small form factor and its pretty look. Her Kindle is collecting dust somewhere in our house. My mentor and friend, Michael Hyatt, also swears by his mini. He takes notes on it, reads on it, and carries it everywhere. He ditched the big iPad; it was too big for him, too clumsy. He simply loves his mini."

Where iPad Mini wins... According to Augusto

"It is not the cool form-factor but the weight. I remember when the iPad 2 came onto the market it was 2.72 ounces lighter (77.11 grams) than the original. The difference wasn't big in numbers but it feels huge when you carry both devices. Lighter will be always be more portable. When we got our first mini, the idea was that we were both going to test it before we made a decision. In the few opportunities that I have been able to grab it, and enjoy the difference of the weight, I really liked it. So much so, that I went ahead and got one for myself. To date, I have been using it as my main iPad. The small screen doesn't bother me as much as I thought it would. Time will tell if it will be a substitute to my main machine or a complement to my setup."

Where the"big" iPad wins... According to Michael

"The screen - it's just bigger and better. The big iPad has a 'Retina screen' - and while it may not mean a lot to an average user, someone like me who got used to no longer seeing pixels on his screen, can't go back to a non-Retina screen. Retina screen simply means, the pixel density on the iPad is so high that a regular eye can't spot any pixel - the text and graphics are extremely sharp and just beautiful to watch. And for someone like me who's working on his iPad all of the time, it makes a difference.

The same applies to the screen real estate. The iPad mini has the same resolution as the big one, but everything is just bigger on the iPad. Again, not a deal breaker for a casual browser but for an #iPadOnly guy like me, it makes all the difference in the world. Especially for the apps that require note-taking, sketching, diagraming, mind-mapping and drawing. Bigger is just better."

Where the "big" iPad wins... According to Augusto

"I have resisted jumping into the Retina iPad because I know that as soon as I began using the better screen the non-retina screen would be an issue. That would mean upgrading way too many machines. So I can't say it is the screen for me, but for me it is typing on the screen.

I can type fast on the screen of the iPad thanks to TapTyping. That allowed me to use the iPad without the external keyboard and to increase my productivity. I have tried to type on the iPad mini and I can't accomplish as much. I may (or may not) improve with practice, but without a doubt it is one area where the bigger iPad wins. I'm not only able to type for longer periods of time using the regular iPad, but I am also much more comfortable.

Since I spend most of my day looking at the screen of the iPad, having more text on the screen it is helpful. That it is one of the reasons I use an external keyboard – to get more screen real estate. That said, the few tests I have performed with the iPad mini prove that in portrait mode I am able to see enough text to be useful.

After a little over a week with the iPad mini, I continue to believe that real estate is an important factor, but weight and portability may take a place in the equation."

Michael's verdict: it depends (duh!)

"I'd say as a secondary device I'd go with the mini. My wife works on a regular PC at work, on a MacBook Air at home and uses the mini as a content-consumption device. As a primary device for #iPadOnly work I'd go with the original iPad - the big one. To me cutting my screen real estate from 13 inches on the MacBook Air to 10 inches on the iPad was already a big deal... and as I work 8-10 hours a day on the iPad, I prefer the big, sharp screen of the big iPad."

Augusto's verdict: I think like the Mini

"Before I got the iPad mini, my answer was the "big" iPad. However after only a week of testing the mini I'm starting to change my mind. My original plan was to have the "big" iPad as the main machine and the iPad mini as a secondary device but the roles are reversed now. I use the mini as my main #iPadOnly computer and I love its reduced size and weight."

The Final Verdict:

The decision as you see comes to weight vs. screen size. From a capability point of view both machines will do the job. In the end it will depend on what you think it is more important to you. At this time, Michael is choosing screen size and Augusto seems inclined to choose weight.

www.youtube.com/iPadOnlyBook

Video #7: Critical element when getting a computer.

CHAPTER #3
THE NEW OFFICE

"Work is not a place to go, it's a thing you do" - Anonymous

Once upon a time there was this idea that you needed a whole office floor or building with a set of expensive tools and powerful mainframe computers in order to have a successful business. Not anymore. You can telecommute and use a regular computer or even better, an iPad that can be powerful enough to get your job done.

In the same way the Blackberry mobile terminal changed the way people were dealing with email on the go, the old office paradigm that made Dilbert so famous is also gone.

Part of the reason to have an office was to have a place for people to meet and exchange ideas and try to maximize the use of expensive equipment. These days, technology is no longer expensive. The cost of a scanner, fax, copier and printer are negligible. The reality is that with the right set of tools you can create a productive work environment anywhere you want and people will be even more effective there than in a regular office.

Augusto lives in the US and Michael in Europe. We've never met in person yet we wrote this book together. The same applies to the way we work with our teams. People who work with us are located in various cities throughout the world. We primarily communicate via email and text messages, and once in a while we use Skype or FaceTime to talk to each other. There is no need to have a place to meet, no need to travel to be able to work together and do what we do. We don't even know at what time people work and if they are sitting sipping piña coladas as they accomplish their work. We care only that the stuff gets done and in a timely manner. That's all that matters anyway.

Michael has always been teleworking and he works in a real office only when he is visiting his friends' offices. He works from home and his 'home office'. He finished his college degree with a thesis on teleworking and virtual teams. All throughout his studies his dream has always been to be able to work from anywhere, with just a laptop and an Internet connection. Nothing else. Today, he is running a very successful Internet-based company (Nozbe) and managing his multi-national team of 15 people on an iPad with a cellular connection. Michael can virtually work from anywhere. And he does. His iPad is his office.

Augusto used to work in a real office with doors and in a cubicle. In 2006 he began working as a teleworker. His office was in a bag. Like Michael, once he experienced that freedom, he didn't want to go back. He has been trying to work independently ever since. One of the differences between Michael and Augusto is that he never managed to set up his home office - he still loves his 'office in a bag'.

www.youtube.com/iPadOnlyBook

Video #8: The office - the past, present... and the future with the iPad.

Michael's "no real office" story

"I started my first company right after college and proclaimed I'd never need an actual office to get my work done. Everyone who knew me told me I could say so because my company was just me. I was the owner, employer and only employee. People said I'd need to get an office when I start hiring. Or when I got my first serious strategic customer.

Both things happened. I got my first, serious customer. They were a Spanish company based in Madrid and I was living in Poland. Two thousand miles apart. Why would I need an office for a customer who'd never visit me? I visited them instead. Great excuse for traveling to Spain on business a few times a year!

I hired my first employee to help serve my 'strategic' customer. She was from Warsaw, Poland. Three hundred miles away. Why would I need an office for an employee who'd never commute 300 miles?

Today I'm no longer running a consultancy business. I'm running Nozbe - a global productivity suite of applications. We are a small team of 15 people (and growing). Some live in Japan, in the US, in Spain, in Germany and the majority are scattered across Poland. Why would I need an office for this bunch? Where would I set this office up? Who would go there?

'Michael, if you ever decide to rent a fancy office space somewhere, good for you, but don't make me go there' - this is what one of my first employees told me. She stands by it. People keep telling me I'd have to grow up some day and get a proper office. MySQL AB - one of the most successful database software companies in the world - had most of its 300-people team teleworking every day. If they could do it, I didn't think I'd need to grow up either."

Augusto's "Mobile Office"

"I have my own business. I opened it with the idea of never needing another permanent office space to accomplish my work. Today most of my office needs are in my bag. My 'mobile office' can be set up anywhere in the world.

My iPad replaced not only my computer, but also my scanner, fax and file cabinet (for those documents that do not require a hard copy for legal reasons). It took me a while to get to this point.

It was back in 1997 when I created my first 'portable office'. It was an old Samsonite briefcase with an Apple PowerBook 170 and a Palm Pilot Professional. As computer bags were uncommon then, I had to use a lot of foam to protect the PowerBook. This setup allowed me to geek out and work in many places... until my laptop's battery died. My freedom was limited to the length of the power supply cable.

For note taking while I was studying for my MBA, I used My Palm Vx with a keyboard, using a software package called 'Documents to Go'. After my MBA, I was handling sales for Latin America, which once again, required having a portable office. I traveled often those days and my setup became quite complex. I had to carry a Scanner, 2 Laptops (a Tablet PC and a Laptop), paperwork, chargers, and much more. Later I'd replace the Laptop for a Mac and much later the Tablet PC for an iPad.

When I wasn't traveling, I dreamed of working in a proper 'home office'. I tried different setups with proper laptop desks, cables, external screens and everything else but I couldn't get myself to work there. The whole 'home office' setup created too many distractions for me. I tried again when I was writing this book. As I needed my Mac a couple more times, I decided to move the data to a more permanent set up, to create something that looked more like a traditional home office. When I did, after just a few days I discovered that it was exactly what I needed to avoid at all cost. Instead of helping me focus, that traditional set up was actually providing more opportunities to get even more distracted. I had to unassembled my home office. As it turned out, I didn't need one. All I needed was a more effective portable office and the iPad was the perfect companion. By writing this book I discovered that my iPad really is my portable office now. Everything else served as a distraction."

Michael and his "Home Office evolution"

"My home office has evolved in the past few years. It is a recurring theme on my blog. My home office changes about once a year. For many reasons. Either my family relocates, I move to a different room, or I decide to re-decorate the room. Anyway, the result is that every year I have a different home office. I provide a guided tour of it on my blog for my readers.

Preparing for this chapter, Augusto reviewed my home office blog posts and he pointed out something I had not realized. 'Have you noticed that every year you have fewer gadgets in your home office?', he said.

He was right. Every year I was trimming my home office down to the minimum amount of gadgets I needed to do the office work. When I started I had two laptops, three screens and lots of other gadgets and hardware. Now I have a Mac Mini, an iPad, and an all-in-one printer/scanner. And that's basically it.

The thing is, I'm rarely using my Mac Mini. And I'm using my printer/scanner even less. Every now and then I need it... but now that you can scan using an app on your iPad or iPhone... and that I rarely need to print anything anymore... my iPhone and iPad have become my real office.

While writing this chapter, I'm at my parents' house for the Easter holiday. I brought only my iPad and iPhone. No Mac, no PC, no Printer/scanner. My iPad and iPhone constitute my home office."

Running a business from the iPad

As you can see, we are not kidding. We are running our entire businesses with our iPads. Michael is running a very successful global business with close to 20 team members scattered across three continents and four time-zones. He is a productivity guy who is a business owner, a product manager, a blogger, a writer and a speaker. He does it all on the iPad and he is having the time of his life.

Augusto also runs his business on the iPad. He doesn't have employees but he deals with editors, designers, lawyers and more. He works in English as well as Spanish, in four countries. He is also a productivity guy, a writer, an author, a business owner, a project manager, a blogger, a consultant and a public speaker. He does it all on the iPad, and like Michael, is also having the time of his life.

We didn't switch to the iPad and #iPadOnly life because we wanted to run our businesses less effectively. We wanted to be even more mobile and more productive. We can say that we have accomplished both.

Yes, it's possible to manage a successful company from a home office (or a portable office) and an iPad. We know we can. We are doing it every single day and we are having a blast in the process.

Can you do your job on an iPad?

Now that you know our journey to our 'iPad office' it's time to dig deeper. Let's see if you can work 95% of the time on the iPad and do the job effectively. Who can really go #iPadOnly?

In general, most professionals use their current machines to communicate, to create something, to analyze data, to share something with someone and to browse the web. The iPad can do most of that, albeit a bit differently than a regular PC. The iPad can also easily exchange files and data with a regular computer or a smartphone.

Unless you use proprietary software, or power-hungry software, you will be able to be #iPadOnly at least half of your day, and maybe more. Actually, if you think about it, people are using their mobile phones already around 60% of their working day, even if they haven't consciously noticed it yet. Simply add the iPad to that equation for the 40% of your work and you're working #iPadOnly.

Michael is an entrepreneur running Nozbe so he wears many hats in his job. He writes a lot. As the 'product guy', he designs his product and is in an ongoing discussion with his developers and designers. As the CEO, he creates spreadsheets, presentations, email, IM, calls... and he blogs. He participates in social media and more; he also travels a bit. If the iPad fits his lifestyle, it'll probably fit yours, too.

Augusto began his journey of #iPadOnly as a Sales Manager handling hardware sales from Canada to Argentina. In that job he relied heavily on email, video conferencing, Excel, Word, PowerPoint and an Internet browser for research. As early as 2010 the iPad could do almost all of that, with the exception of video conferencing.

Next, Augusto moved on to his current role as a writer, public speaker and business owner. He is in the business of discovering innovative ideas that can help people do their job better and have a better life. Most of his job is invisible. An important part of his job is to think and look for obscure connections. He spends a great deal of his day reading and writing on his iPad. The other thing he does on his iPad is number crunching within Excel. That's how he tracks his relevant business data.

Again, who can do their job effectively on the iPad?

Here's a list of job descriptions that, in our opinion, are a perfect fit for the #iPadOnly lifestyle. The list is not definitive, but meant to give you an idea. By the way, we won't mention any apps in this chapter as there is a dedicated chapter on apps later in this book. Let's focus on which types of work can be done on the iPad:

1. CEO of a company / Small Business Owner

As CEO and Small Business Owner there is lots of email to process. The iPad has a great email client. We also work with spreadsheets, presentations and word processing - the iPad has great apps for those needs, too. Other than that, we use a project and time management app to communicate through tasks with our team. The iPad has also great apps for social media, chatting and video conferencing. The iPad is a CEO / Small Business Owner powerhouse in a small form factor.

2. Writer

The iPad is perfect for writers as the screen can be used vertically (perfect for typing with an external keyboard) and the one-app-open-at-a-time paradigm keeps the focus on writing thus minimizing distractions. Again, the form factor is crucial as you can carry the iPad in your purse or bag and write anywhere you want.

3. Blogger

Most of the blogging platforms have dedicated blogging apps for the iPad. And great web interfaces. To deal with blog post formatting, many people use the Markdown format to be able to write in plain text and publish richly formatted blog posts. Moreover, iPad has some of the best social media apps available. It is a great social-media-blogger type of machine.

4. Traveler

With ten hours of battery life, half a kg weight, sized to fit any purse (or man-purse, for that matter), the iPad is a fantastic device for traveling. Add dedicated travel apps for flight tracking, hotel booking, navigation and maps, it's hard not to make it the traveler's best friend.

5. Programmer

This is a tricky part. Although Michael continues to do some of the programming for his company, it's not as much as he used to. While researching for this book project he found full-time programmers who code mostly on their iPads so yes, it's more than doable. The same benefits of writing on the iPad apply to coding. Great coding apps are available for the iPad and the work can be done with the iPad in a vertical orientation.

There is an additional benefit of coding on the iPad. When you do, you need to move the server-side (and Git) part of your code to an actual external server rather than installing everything on your local machine. You'll notice it's actually more efficient this way.

AUGUSTO PINAUD & MICHAEL SLIWINSKI

6. Product guy

Michael spends his days designing new features for Nozbe, testing what his programmers and designers have developed and responding with lots of feedback. Thanks to great apps for drawing, sketching and visual design he has fun doing it on the iPad. He bought a stylus that helps him draw and sketch. It's efficient and a lot more fun to design the product and send feedback via the iPad.

7. Busy professional

Well, that's all of us - Michael, Augusto and you - a mixture of the examples above. Our experiment with going #iPadOnly has been a success and we are not going back. We love the fact that we can take our iPads anywhere we want in a small man-purse or bag and nobody really knows we have a real working machine with us at all times. We don't need to search for a power plug as we have more battery than we need for a full day's work. Our iPads sync perfectly with our iPhones through many cloud apps allowing us to be on top of things at all times.

iPad is the new office.

It's our smallest office yet (if you don't count the iPhone). With this chapter we wanted to prove that it can be your office, too. Apart from being more productive, you might be surprised how much fun it really is to work on the iPad.

www.youtube.com/iPadOnlyBook

Video #9: Is working on the iPad radical? How is the iPad better than a laptop?.

Keyboard is optional.

We're used to having keyboards around. All typewriters and early computers had keyboards. The modern computers have keyboards. Our laptops have keyboards. Even early smartphones had them.

Yet when iPhone was unveiled in 2007 by Steve Jobs, he looked at the smartphones category and famously said: "They all have these keyboards, whether you need them or not to be there. And they all have these control buttons that are fixed in plastic and are the same for every application. Well, every application wants a slightly different user interface, a slightly optimized set of buttons just for it."

People didn't get Steve's strong opinion and proclaimed the iPhone as a failure because it didn't have the keyboard. Well, when you look at the phones now, all of them look like an iPhone and they do not have keyboards.

As with the iPhone, on the iPad keyboard is optional.

People complain about the iPad's lack of keyboard and lack of keyboard shortcuts... well, on the iPad the keyboard is optional. The fact you can interact with your data in a more natural and intimate way is a big advantage, especially if you're like us and work many hours a day in front of your computer.

Again, if you want to work on the iPad in the same way you do on your desktop or laptop computer, you will be disappointed. It doesn't work like that. There is a fun aspect that the touch and intimacy produces with your work that helps you enjoy interacting with this machine.

Do you really need the keyboard all that much?

Michael was working on his MacBook Air over the recent years and he loved it - the form, size, weight, the quality of the back-lit keyboard... except for the fact that this great keyboard was attached to his Air whether he needed it or not. He found he didn't need the keyboard to browse the web, play music, read articles, ebooks or PDFs. He realized he hardly used the keyboard when he was sending feedback to his team. He preferred to visually design interfaces for his app, working with mind-maps and managing tasks and projects in Nozbe. He only needed the keyboard for the task it was always designed for - writing. Other than that, he found himself using the Air keyboard less and less.

When Augusto moved from the TabletPC to the MacBook, one of the things that he missed was the fact that he could turn the machine, and place the keyboard on the back, out of the way, unless he really wanted to use it. Like Michael, he rarely uses the keyboard when he is not writing.

Another thing is the user interface of the apps - on the Mac you either have to use the keyboard shortcuts or move the mouse cursor around. On the iPad you just tap around; it's faster and more intuitive.

The keyboard is still important, but with the rise of Siri and her dictation software (improving with each iOS release) and gesture-based navigation, the keyboard is only needed when you need to type something of length. Other than that, it's not necessary. When using the iPad we need to forget the traditional keyboard shortcuts (Ctrl+Alt+Del anyone?) and all the PC-era things and focus on the new. It takes some time getting used to, but we love the new experience

The keyboard is only an "addition" and not the "main part" of the iPad.

The first time you pick up the iPad and touch the virtual keyboard you find it unresponsive, awkward and cumbersome to type on. And it takes up half of the screen. At first, neither of us liked it.
However, as soon as you are willing to question the assumptions and learn a new way to type you will be surprised how much you can actually get done with the iPad's on-screen keyboard and how fast you can type.

The on-screen keyboard is a lot different from the regular one - there is no feedback (unless you like the click sound that came as the default - we hate it). It is smaller and is configured differently than a PC keyboard. If you are expecting those things to be the same, the keyboard on the screen will never work for you.

On-screen keyboard tricks.

As soon as you let go of your old assumptions, you will

discover how fast you can type. For example, did you know that if you are typing on the screen keyboard and need to type a quotation mark there is more than one way to accomplish that? You can hit the [.?123] button and then hit the ["] or you can place your finger on the [?.] key and swipe it upward. The same applies to ['] - just swipe up on the [!,] key. When you finish a sentence, just hit Spacebar twice and you'll see a dot and a space. And there are more tricks like that.

Keyboard shortcuts to the rescue.

Finally with iOS5, the keyboard shortcuts came to the iPad and iPhone... and with iOS6 and the iCloud they are synced across all the devices. This means when you define a new keyboard shortcut, it's synced between your iPad and the iPhone - available for use on both!

We learned to define some very cool keyboard shortcuts that allow us to type less every day. Michael likes to add his email address by just typing 'xm' and his email address appears. Augusto has links for his books, so by typing 'w4amen' the address for the book on Amazon shows up.

Keyboard shortcuts come in handy when we are answering emails quickly. We've defined 'Best Regards,' by just typing 'br'. To say 'Thanks for your email and really sorry for my late reply!' Michael types 'tfs'. To say 'You are welcome!' Augusto types yaw!, to type his address he types '.address' and Michael types 'adh'. And we've got many, many more.

The fact is we have been trained to type on our keyboards way too much.

When you think about it, keyboard shortcuts don't come pre-installed on any desktop operating system. We tend to type a lot more on 'normal' computers. On any given day, count the number of times you type your email address. Now count the number of mistakes you made. See what we mean?

On our iPads, we have a rule that whenever there is a phrase we catch ourselves typing twice on a given day, we go to system Settings and make a shortcut for it. This works like magic. Now the key is to make the shortcuts very easy to remember and as short as possible. Now if there were only a shortcut to get to 'Settings > General > Keyboard > Shortcuts > Add new' in just one or two taps that would be a different story. Why Apple buried this feature so deep in the system is beyond us.

There are even apps for longer shortcuts and templates.

Michael uses an app called TextExpander that allows him to define longer, multi-line shortcuts. The downside is, it only works in supported apps, and it is the reason Augusto doesn't use it in email (it doesn't work in Apple Mail). However it does work in the apps he uses for writing (Byword, Nebulous, AI Writer) and it's a great way of preparing longer 'templates' of texts. When Michael types 'msblog' an entire template of his blog post is pasted into his document. A super time-saver.

You can touch-type on the on-screen keyboard.

This came as a surprise to both of us. We're both touch-typists, meaning we use all of our fingers to type and we never look at the keyboard as we type - our fingers 'know' where the keys are. Augusto can type 80-100 words per minute (WPM) and Michael, 60-80. If you've never learned to touch-type, stop reading this book and start today. Augusto, in his best-selling book: '25 Tips for Productivity' challenges everyone to measure their typing speed and take some touch-typing classes. Just think about it, after a month of training you can be typing up to three times faster than you do now. Instead of writing a long email in ten minutes, you'll have it done in a little over three. It's the single most effective way to reclaim 2-3 hours off your work time per week.

Back to the iPad. Thanks to his friend's recommendation, Augusto learned of an app called TapTyping for the iPad and the iPhone that teaches you to touch-type on the on-screen keyboard. He recommended the app to Michael. Suddenly, instead of writing 20-30 WPM on the iPad's on-screen keyboard, Augusto reached speeds of more than 60 WPM and Michael, 50 WPM. This simply means they now type almost as fast on the on-screen keyboard as they do on a regular one. Now that's an improvement!

We do use external keyboards for writing longer texts.

That's right, here's Michael's take on it:

"When I'm not writing a book, a blog post, an article or any other longer piece of text, I don't use the external keyboard. When I process my email Inbox to zero, I tap on emails and write using the on-screen keyboard... and when I switched to the iPad I learned to reply to emails quicker. I practice 5-sentence replies (usually less) and move on to the next email message. I know I'm not being as polite as I used to be but over the years I've found out people preferred a quicker reply than a nicer one. With email, speed is what matters most.

When writing long passages of text (like this chapter) I move to an external keyboard. When I started my #iPadOnly journey I bought the 'ZaggFlex Keys' keyboard and I loved it. Later I switched to the Logitech Ultrathin Keyboard as it also works as an iPad cover and enables me to write on my lap.

What I love about writing on my iPad's external keyboard is the fact that I can put the iPad in a vertical position. Writing on a vertical screen feels more natural than on the horizontal screen of a laptop. It feels like writing on letter-sized paper. I have my writing app open and it occupies my entire iPad screen - I see my words and nothing else. With an external keyboard and in vertical mode, the iPad is the ultimate writer's machine."

Here's what Augusto thinks about his keyboard:

"I like full size keyboards, and I believe that you need to use the best tool for the job at hand. Sometimes, that means a full size keyboard and in my opinion the physical keyboard is better for longer typing.

First of all there is the angle, my wrist gets tired typing on the iPad screen, and as a writer I need to make sure that I take good care of those parts of my body that are key to my profession.

Second, I like to see more than a paragraph at the time, and when you use the onscreen keyboard you lose around half of the real estate for the keyboard alone.

Third, I love the fact that with the iPad you have the option to place it in Portrait or Landscape mode. Depending on what you are writing it is something very handy to be able to do. Try doing *that* with your laptop!

Fourth, When I type on the screen I can't maintain good posture; I end up in pain if I type on the screen for more than two hours.

Fifth, When I write I love to use the black screen with white text. It is much softer on my eyes, and eye strain is something I do everything in my power to avoid.

Sixth, I can type much faster and I like the feeling of the full size keyboard. The amount of text I create on a regular basis makes and external keyboard the best tool for the job."

The keyboard is an accessory - it's not the iPad's main thing

Again, iPad is a post-PC device where the keyboard appears only when it's needed, but most of the time, it's out of the way. That's how we treat it and that's how we learned to work.

Switching to the iPad made us re-think the way we work and the amount of typing we did on the laptop simply because the keyboard was so readily available! Well, not anymore.

Michael tries to type less and enjoy computing more. Sometimes he is slower because of the on-screen keyboard, but most of the times he is also happier, because he is not typing as much as he used to. And that's the whole point of working more efficiently, right?

Augusto feels exactly the same. Except for the books, he types less and less and is able to think, interact and spend his time doing what it is really important.

It's hard to make the switch! It was hard for us, but it was definitely worth it.

Productivity on the iPad.

With the iPad and our #iPadOnly work we're constantly questioning the traditional assumptions related to the computers. In the last chapter we talked about the keyboard and why it's actually not a bad idea to question the fact that we need it so much to get our job done. Next, let's deal with other great benefits of the iPad and what really makes it a great productivity-boosting machine.

If we look into the dictionary, productivity is defined as 'the quality of being productive or having the power to produce'. This is where the iPad shines - it gives you the ability to accomplish much in a compact shape and form. It doesn't matter if you use an iPad or an iPad Mini, the device has the power to bring you more than its size indicates.

Instantaneous - the barrier of entry is low.

Traditional computers are fast and powerful but very often getting to the point of performing a task requires a long process. You have to start the computer, log in, wait until your desktop shows up, find an appropriate application, or better yet, find an appropriate file first, start it, dive in... this all takes time.

With the iPad you have fewer steps... and most of all; all of them are very fast. You pick up the iPad, swipe to unlock, go to the app and dive into work. There is virtually no time gap between each of these steps. Everything is near instantaneous even though the iPad, in theory, has a slower processor than your desktop computer. It just feels a lot faster... thus helping you get things done easier. You will find that the perceived speed of accessing tasks creates a lower 'barrier of entry' and will help you achieve your goals.

Focus - your ultimate ally.

Thanks to the iPad's one-app-at-a-time paradigm, once you've fired up your desired app and started to perform your task there is nothing to distract you from doing it. There is no 'other window' tempting you to switch to it. Your current window is the only place you work. I found it very liberating on the iPad. No distractions.

Even more so in writing apps like Byword, Nebulous or AI Writer where all you see is your text on your screen. Nothing more. No bells, whistles, or buttons. Everything just goes away. As Augusto would say - your only options are to write or not to write. To perform your task, or not.

Here's how Augusto puts it:

"I work at home. My 4 year old goes to school from 8:30 to 12:30. Our new baby (he was born in February 2013) requires my constant attention. On top of that I have a business to take care of, books that I am writing, books that I am selling, and a household that my wife and I take care of. My daughter also participates in gymnastics, ballet and takes Spanish lessons. All of this requires that we move in synchronicity in order to accomplish all the important stuff as quickly as possible.

The iPad provided me with a productivity boost that a laptop never could. On the PC I constantly had too many options on my screen and was easily distracted. Being #iPadOnly gives me the ability to focus when I need to, to shift focus when I need to, to produce when I need to and so on and so forth."

Switching away is also fast.

As with anything - what works to your advantage can work to

your disadvantage. Because everything happens so quickly on the iPad, switching to a social media app or movie-watching app on the iPad is equally quick so the temptation to just 'click for a second to check something else' can rule over you and tempt you to go somewhere and spend the next hour browsing, reading and enjoying yourself, totally forgetting about your task at hand. The single app on the screen paradigm helps you stay in the zone, to forget about your task and dive in without clicking and browsing.

Ultimately it's all about discipline and focus... but what we found on the iPad over the last year is that both are easier to find. The design of the iPad helps you get to your tasks quickly and find the focus you need to perform them efficiently.

Another factor that helps the iPad become the ultimate productivity machine is its flexibility of the device itself. The key lies in the hardware design of the iPad.

The keyboard.

As mentioned in the last chapter, the keyboard on the iPad is totally optional. It's only there when it plays a crucial role in accomplishing a certain task. Otherwise, when you're reading, for instance, it disappears off the screen.

The optional keyboard boosts productivity as it doesn't get in the way of what you're doing. It assists you when you need it and is tucked away when you don't. Throughout our last year of working on the iPad we have both managed to design our workflows in such a way that we're using the keyboard less and less each day. Less typing. More action. More tapping. More things done.

Horizontal? Vertical? Depends on the task...

With the traditional computers you're forced to use the screen in a horizontal view. Previously, laptops had a 4:3 screen ratio, the same as the current iPad. But now, because of movies, the screens are more like a 16:9 ratio... which leaves you with a screen that is very wide, but not very high. Apart from having the 4:3 ratio, the iPad is again, very flexible - you can rotate it anyway you want.

We wrote this book with the iPad in a vertical view – which feels very natural for writing. When watching a movie you can easily switch the iPad to horizontal view. To read the news you can go vertical again, to check email go horizontal... well, you get the idea. Depending on the task at hand and the app you're currently using you can hold the iPad in either direction.

In fact, there really is no 'right' way to hold it. You can hold it upside down (with the 'home' button at the top) and the screen will rotate 180 degrees. Just pick up the iPad and the screen rotates to the best orientation depending on gravity. This makes the iPad the most flexible computer ever - you don't have to think about 'how to' pick it up - just take it and use it..

Form factor and the size - even more productive.

When talking about which way to hold your iPad - the sheer fact that you can hold it is great. It's not a bulky laptop or an enormous desktop machine. And it fits into a purse so you can virtually take it anywhere you want.

Most laptops weigh between 3-7 lbs (1.5-3kg) Well, the iPad is only 1lb (0,5kg). It's light. You can take it anywhere. Even if you don't travel with it, working or reading on it within your house is very easy. Its flexibility increases productivity because, again - the barrier of entry is very low. Want to catch up on reading in the kitchen while waiting for the potatoes to boil? Take the iPad with you. Hold it. Read. Enjoy :-)

Touching is magic, more natural and fun.

One of my favorite songs of all time is Phil Collins 'Jesus, He Knows Me' and at the end of the song Phil is shouting: 'Touch the screen, heal!' - Well, this is how I feel working on the iPad.

We are humans. We have senses and one of these is the sense of touch. We love touching things and people. When you touch someone it means you care about them, that's why you see couples walking holding each other's hands. We also appreciate touching quality materials and fabrics. We enjoy touching wooden desks, silk shirts, and the iPad or iPhone's aluminum and glass finish. That's why Apple is so crazy about the materials they use for building their products.

Michael still repeats his story of enchantment with the first Macbook Air he bought. He says it was an amazing experience to touch the aluminum enclosure of his new computer after having spent years working with plastic laptops like the IBM ThinkPad or Toshiba Portage. He says he simply fell in love with the new laptop because of the quality of the materials it was made with.

Gestures are really fun.

After decades of touching the keyboard we're finally touching a lot more when working on the iPad. We can actually touch email! We can also use gestures in many apps. We can swipe tasks to complete them! We can pinch and zoom on a map to view it in more detail!

In the iPad's Settings you can enable four-finger gestures like 'pinch to go to home screen' (which is a lot cooler than searching for the 'home' button), 'swipe up to see the multi-tasking pane' (again, no need to double-tap the 'home button') or 'swipe left or right to switch between apps'.

It's all kind of magical and it doesn't get tiring. We should know, we've been working on the iPad for more than a year now and we still love every minute of it. The sense of touch is back again.

Touching content on the iPad's screen feels natural, feels great and is more fun. We both believe that when work is more fun, you're more productive. You enjoy working and suddenly work becomes a part of a game. You play while working on the iPad.

The battery lasts forever.

Our first laptops had close to 2 hours of battery life. Even then, because of the speed of the machine it was more like 35-45 working minutes. Later it improved to 3 hours; with an extended battery, 4 hours. Later still, the MacBook Air came with 6-7 hours of battery life. Augusto remembers that his HP tablet also had a forever battery that gave him 6 extra hours of battery, extending the total battery life to almost 10 hours. The weight of that battery was another 3-4 kilos - a high price to pay for a full day of battery life. Now with the iPad we get 10 hours of battery life easily. It's more than you need for a full day's work. For much less weight.

Michael still remembers his "laptop battery" problems:

"I remember traveling with my laptop and making sure to leave home with the battery fully charged. When entering a cafeteria or at the airport I'd constantly seek a place to plug in my laptop to re-charge it. I remember being crazy mad at people occupying spots near the power outlets without using them! How outrageous!

With my iPad as my main machine, I laugh at these situations. I rarely take my power charger with me. I leave it home unless I'm traveling overnight. Then, all I have to remember is to charge my iPad during the night. In the morning, my iPad is fully charged, backed up through iCloud in the process, and ready for the new day.

The iPad's power indicator shows 100% at the beginning but what the iPad is actually saying to me is this: - '10 hours of usage, Michael'. It sounds trivial, but when at the end of the day I have 20% of juice left, I don't freak out. On the laptop, I'd start searching for a power source; while on the iPad it means I have 2 full hours of productivity ahead of me. Two full hours! This usually happens around 5 or 6 pm when I'm finishing my work - it's still enough power to read for half an hour and watch an hour of my favorite show before going to sleep and recharging my iPad."

There is no doubt the great battery life makes the iPad a very productive device. You don't have to worry about searching for power outlets or about schlepping your charger with you. You can just work and get things done... and laugh silently at the guys sitting on the floor in the airport terminal connected to some distant power outlet with their long cables...

We are not an exception.

We can understand that some people will claim that we can go #iPadOnly because we don't work in offices or we don't have bosses or this or that. Nope. We're not that special.

Michael is running his successful business with an iPad. His team of 20 co-workers are scattered across the globe and time zones. Augusto wrote four books and translated six from English to Spanish, all on his iPad. These numbers don't include this book, which of course has also been written by both of us on the iPad.

Yet people still wonder how we can be working #iPadOnly. They don't notice that they are doing a lot of work on their iPhones or other smartphones. They don't notice that a lot of those tasks could be done on an iPad, but instead they convince themselves that they really need a powerful computer to get their tasks done.

The reality is that most people can be #iPadOnly if they are willing to evaluate their needs and workflow, as well as work on their assumptions. If you think that's not the case, think about all of the things about your current setup and workflows that are not as productive as you wish they could be. Then think on what the perfect productivity image would be ('the end in mind')... then think for a moment how the iPad can provide you a better solution. The more you move towards the iPad thinking on a productive workflow, the more you will discover how productive you could be.

www.youtube.com/iPadOnlyBook

Video #10: The iPad as a productivity machine - why do we get more done on the iPad?.

CHAPTER #4
#IPADONLY EVERY DAY - THE APPS, THE WORKFLOWS AND EVERYTHING IN BETWEEN!

When we started our #iPadOnly journey we heard people laugh at the idea of working and managing our businesses entirely on the iPad. However, with each passing month we noticed less and less people thinking it was impossible and more and more starting to question how this can be done. More people are discovering that for far too long they were forced to believe that the only way to accomplish work was in a certain office environment, with a specific kind of software and on a 'serious' kind of computer. People started asking themselves if they could go #iPadOnly, too, when they noticed that the iPad goes with places a laptop never could.

Others get amazed that anyone can work full or most of the time on the iPad. They assume that it is because of a specific kind of a job they do. When Andy Ihnatko, Harry McCracken, James Kendrick, Shane Pearlman, David Kassan, Margaret Manning, Frasier Speirs, Richard Bowman or Richie Hawtin work constantly or mostly #iPadOnly many people argue that it is because of what they do for a living. That's not really the case as on that list we have writers, bloggers, CEOs, painters, teachers, physicians, musicians/DJs... and we know of many more specialists who turn to their iPads as their main machines.

We believe the post-PC revolution is real and the regular PCs will only be 'trucks' used by the few. People will start using not only iPads, but also other tablets based on Android or Windows platforms to get their jobs done. However, the iPad definitely has a head-start and is a more mature platform in terms of tablet-specific apps. The iPad apps are very polished and designed to take advantage of the iPad's big multi-touch screen.

The main goal of this chapter is to show you our #iPadOnly lifestyle in detail. We start each section of this chapter with a job that needs to be done and show which apps we use to make it all happen. You will see in practice what works for us and which kind of workflows we built to make our #iPadOnly journey as effective as possible.

Thanks to the fact that this book has two authors, you'll get a chance to see how both of us work and soon you'll notice we use different apps and have different workflows to achieve the same objectives. This is the longest chapter of the book, but it will show you the nitty gritty of #iPadOnly. This is where the rubber meets the road. This is the most practical part of the book where we reveal all of our secrets and show you how we use our iPads every single day to get everything done..

www.youtube.com/iPadOnlyBook

Video #11: Designing Workflows for an effective and productive iPad-only work.

Web Browsing.

The iPad is much better at web browsing than a laptop or a smartphone. By tapping to open the links, swiping to scroll up and down the page, double tapping to zoom in and out, pinching, swiping left and right... browsing on the iPad feels magical. It feels like you're touching the Internet.

This is what the iPad was created for - to be your 'touch-terminal' to the Internet. And we believe they did an amazing job. Both of us prefer browsing through web pages on the iPad rather than any other machine. It just feels right.

Apple wants you to use Safari to browse the web.

Safari is the default web browser on the iPad. According to Apple it's the best browser on the iPad as they won't let you change your default browser to anything else. There are other browsers on the iPad but Apple forces them to use the same web-browsing engine (iOS Webkit) so they don't seem to be that different. But they are. And the other browsers are really cool. Especially since Safari on the iPad cannot have plug-ins, meaning, you cannot add too much additional functionality to it.

Augusto prefers to use two different browsers

Augusto uses two browsers, one for work (Chrome) and one for play (Safari). Both sync with the iPhone and the Mac and allow him to keep focus on work and play where appropriate.

Bookmarklet

Well, you can kind of add functionality to the default Safari browser through 'Bookmarklets'. A Bookmarklet is a special script that can be saved to Bookmarks and instead of taking you to a web site like the traditional Bookmark does, it launches a special script that helps you get something done.

A few examples: Pocket as well as Instapaper are the apps we use for 'saving articles to read later' (more on that in another chapter) and both offer a Bookmarklet. When you're visiting a web site on the iPad and you click on the Bookmark bar and then on the Pocket or Instapaper Bookmarklet, it saves this page in the app for 'reading later'. Evernote, as well as Nozbe, have similar Bookmarklets. Nozbe adds a web site as a task and Evernote clips the web site as a note. Bookmarklet is a very cool 'hack' that improves Safari's functionality without modifying the browser. All you do is just save a piece of code as your Bookmark.

1Password

There are some things you can't do with Bookmarklets. Even though Safari can prompt you to save passwords, we don't like the way it handles this and we feel we need more control. This is when we turn to 1Password.

We hate remembering passwords. Also, the ones we can remember are not necessarily secure or difficult. 1Password does a much better job at remembering and creating good ones. We store all of our passwords and confidential information in the 1Password app. 1Password also helps creating secure passwords and you can define how long you want it to be, whether or not to use digits, symbols and much more.

The latest version of this app is universal and it works on both our iPhones and our iPads. There is also a desktop version for the Mac and PC and they all sync together via Dropbox or iCloud.

It's one thing to store passwords, and another thing use them in everyday work. The Safari browser is very limited in this regard. As mentioned, you cannot add plug-ins or add-ons to Safari in any way. We were used to browsing the web on the Mac and having a 1Password plugin ready. When we needed to log in to some site, we'd click on the 1Password plugin and it'd fill out the info for us.

Now on the iPad the situation is actually reversed. The 1Password app has a web browser built in. You click on the 1Password app and open a web browsing window and navigate to any site you want. And when you want to log in somewhere, just tap on the navigation bar and you're logged in!

It's very easy and convenient. This also creates a secure environment. To go to an online banking site just go to 1Password and log in there. It feels like a closed and secured silo that keeps the information safe from anyone else.
If you're serious about your password security you should use 1Password to store the confidential information there and browse to particularly sensitive web sites from within it as well.

Other Browsers we sometimes turn to:

Mercury Browser or Google Chrome

Both have great 'private browsing' mode - useful for visiting sites you don't really trust. After you close the browser all the private info like history, cookies, etc., all trace of your browsing is gone.

The other cool thing about these browsers is the fact that you can set up the 'user agent' as Mac/Safari instead of the iPad. Some sites are designed very well for the iPad. When they detect the iPad they offer a very nice browsing experience, other sites put the iPad in the 'mobile camp' and show the same tiny web site they have optimized for the iPhone. Well, iPad IS NOT an iPhone and it has a much bigger screen. Moreover, most of these sites have no way of 'switching' to the 'desktop web site'. This is when Mercury Browser or Chrome shine as they can basically 'lie' to the web sites and identify the iPad as a Mac.

Puffin Browser

Back in the day there was a big battle between Apple and Adobe on why the iOS devices didn't support a technology called 'Flash'. It's an old technology and HTML5 is better (at least that's what Apple is saying). However, Flash used to be very popular and there are still websites built entirely using Flash. That's where Puffin browser comes in - it allows you to browse Flash built web sites - it's slow, but it gets the job done.

www.youtube.com/iPadOnlyBook
Video #12: Browsing on the iPad with 1Password app.

How the iPad changed 'web browsing' activity

A web browser on the iPad is still important but the iPad has dramatically altered the way we browse the Internet. Want to visit the IMDB? Amazon? Ikea? BBC? CNN? Techcrunch? Well, you can but when you're #iPadOnly you don't browse via the Internet, you download their apps to browse their content.

This is another cool thing of the iPad. When you're on a traditional computer, to read these sites you'd have to go to their WWW web sites - no other choice. On the iPad you get their apps from the App Store and interact with them through the app. It's much better. Like a different league. Here are some of the benefits:

1) No more bookmarks - just the home screen. There is no need to bookmark the sites. No need to write their web addresses - they are right on the home screen. Just one tap away. Michael actually keeps them all in a 'Browse' folder on his iPad. It's so convenient.

2) They look better - The apps are usually written from the ground up. They're not just the sites wrapped around an 'app frame' - they are totally new apps, usually designed by new designers who take a fresh look at the site's content, optimize the experience to the iPad's screen and gestures... and the result is pretty amazing.
Have a look at the IMDB web site. It's always been pretty ugly and for a movie freak like Michael, it was annoying. Now on the iPad, it's a totally different ball game - now the app is his ultimate water cooler. He loves browsing it, learning about the movies, actors... and watching movie trailers.

3) The apps work better - most of these apps use gestures like swiping, scrolling, tapping, tap-and-holding, flipping and the like. It's a lot more than you can do on a web site. It's just fun and addictive. The web sites work better on the iPad thanks to their native apps.

The era of 'appification'

The 'appification' of the web redefines the way we interact with the content on the Internet. To Michael, it's another benefit of using the iPad on a daily basis. Thanks to the ever-increasing number of web sites that turn to apps we can literally 'touch the Internet' and interact with the web on a whole new level. Additionally, the iPad's big screen enables us to appreciate the web content even more.

When Steve Jobs introduced the iPad he was so right - the iPad is significantly better at browsing the web than a personal computer or a smartphone. After more than a year of our #iPadOnly journey, we can't highlight this enough.

Reading.

Obviously reading it is a big part of what the iPad will allow you to do in a very convenient way. You've got Newsstand, iBooks, Kindle and many other applications that will allow you to read magazines, books and much more content directly on the iPad.

Amazon Kindle

Let's start with the Amazon Kindle and the Kindle app on the iPad.

Here's Augusto's take:

"I remember when I got my first ebook. It was 1998 and it was a book that I read on the Palm Pilot. I knew then that I didn't want to read another paper book ever again. I met this revolution head-on. I read on all of my devices, including the iPad. I bought four Kindles, and honestly until the Kindle Paperwhite came out, my preferred device to read was the iPad. But I fell in love with the backlighted e-ink screen and ever since, I have been reading much more there than on the iPad."

Michael's take:

"I love the Kindle as an idea - to get ebooks to your device, over the air, just when you want them. In my family we've owned all the Kindle models (my wife used to love them) and yet, I still prefer to read on the iPad. As I said, my wife loved her Kindle device... until she got her iPad mini. Now we both read on the iPad only. The Kindle devices are now collecting dust. The only drawback I see to the Kindle iPad app is the fact that you have to go to the Kindle Store web site on the iPad to get new books. I'd love to have it in the app, but obviously Amazon doesn't want to pay Apple 30% commission on each book sold."

Overdrive

Augusto also uses an application called Overdrive that allows him to get eBooks from the Public Library. The selection isn't big, but once in a while works like a charm.

Other eBook apps

There are other applications like the Nook or Kobo, but in the end on our devices we use iBooks, Kindle and (in Augusto's case) Overdrive. We buy most of the books in the Kindle Store and some of them on iBooks.

Advantages of reading eBooks on the iPad

One of the cool things of reading electronically is the ability to increase the font size as you start to tire; that usually allows you to read for a couple of more hours. Also, you can read on black background with white text. In our experience, this is much easier on the eyes.
If all that it is not enough, you also have access to dictionaries and can carry with you an infinite collection of books.

Amazon Kindle storage

There's more - Amazon gives you 5GB of space for your documents in their 'Amazon cloud'. Michael uses it for his PDFs:

"Before the iPad I used to collect many PDFs but never got around to reading any of them. I had many folders with many PDFs hidden deep in my laptop. Thanks to Amazon's Kindle -

that workflow has changed as well. I send PDFs to my Kindle. Every Kindle device has an individual email address. Just go to your Kindle app on the iPad and check in 'Settings'. Now, add this email address to your contacts.

Every time someone sends me a PDF version of a book or a chapter of a book... or I receive a PDF worth reading through Dropbox or any other sharing app... I forward the PDF via email to my Kindle. This way the PDF is uploaded to the Kindle cloud and is available on all of my devices. It's also automatically downloaded on my iPad. I now have many choices available as to where I'd like to read it – iPad, iPhone, or my Kindle.

Thanks to going #iPadOnly I'm no longer saving PDFs in many different places or taking time to think about where I should save them... I send them all to the Kindle Cloud... and with 5GB of space offered by Amazon, there's still lots of space before it fills up."

iBooks

Even with the investment we've made over the years in our numerous Kindle books, we can't ignore the presence and importance of iBooks as an ebook reader application. Apple has come a long way to not only make their application useful but also really cool.

They created an accompanying software suite called iBooks Author that allows writers to create very interactive books. This book is an example of it. If you are reading this book on any other platform than iBooks you need to go the website we created for you to access the special videos we recorded for you. However, if you are reading this in iBooks on the iPad you are going to be able to watch the videos right within this book.

This new breed of interactive and iPad-friendly ebooks, that basically look and work like apps, makes the iBooks platform very appealing. That is the reason we decided to publish our #iPadOnly book in this new format.

Google Reader and Reeder or Mr Reader... and Feedly.

We are bloggers and we like to read other blogs, too. We used to use Google Reader web app to aggregate all of the blogs we read. Unfortunately, by the time you are reading this, Google has shut down this service.

Michael's RSS reader of choice until now was the Reeder app. It is a fantastic app for reading blogs. The interface is beautiful and makes heavy use of swiping gestures. It's a joy to use, especially on the iPad in the vertical position. In addition, Reeder integrates with great apps like Evernote, Pocket and others - to easily share the most interesting posts with other apps.

As you'll see from the next chapters there is a specific workflow that Michael has which starts with Reeder, goes to Pocket and then to Evernote and other apps and places.
Anyway - Reeder was his RSS and blog reader of choice and most of the content he consumed on the iPad started with this app.

Augusto believes Mr Reader to be the best RSS reader that he has ever found. He loves the fact that you can see the feed directly in so many formats (RSS, Web, Instapaper, Reader and Pocket), you can access Google folders, create as well organize them and interact with Google Reader without the need to interact with the Google's web application. The sharing abilities of the application are amazing. It allows you to select the link, the title, some of the text, send to Instapaper, share on Facebook or Twitter... It is really a complete solution.

However, because Google is shutting down their Reader web app and because both of our favorite RSS readers are based on it and still haven't come up with a solution to help us migrate our RSS feeds, we already started using a new kid on the block - the application called Feedly. Altogether, it's a very well done app. It currently syncs with Google Reader but they've written their own syncing mechanism so even when Google shuts down their service, we can continue to read our RSS feeds like we used to. The gestures and the whole 'reading flow' is a little different on Reeder or Mr Reader, but we're getting used to it and we're thankful someone decided to build a solution that helped us seamlessly migrate from Google Reader.

"Read it later" apps like Instapaper and Pocket

Especially if you're using your iPad as a media and content consumption device, you will appreciate this new breed of apps that help you save web pages and blog posts for later allowing you to read them comfortably within these apps. As a bonus, the content you save for later is being parsed by these apps and re-formatted so that you don't see the entire web site but just the article you're interested in.

Apple also built this functionality within their Safari in the form of a 'Reading list' but both Michael and Augusto prefer to use more advanced, stand-alone apps for this purpose.

Augusto and the Instapaper app:

"Instapaper is one of these applications that I really enjoy and use daily on the iPad and the iPhone. The idea behind the app is that you save articles from the web and later, you read them offline; without the noise on the page, additional ads and graphics.

I am so used to Instapaper that if I am on the go and find a link that I want to read and the page is 'polluted' (meaning, it has heavy graphics and other distracting content), I send it to the Instapaper and read it there immediately. Fast. Clean. Efficient.

The problem, of course, is that you can fill the Instapaper inbox rapidly. I have been forced to learn to treat the Instapaper Inbox as that, an inbox. Instapaper allows you to create folders, and after the articles land in the Instapaper inbox, they get processed into folders. There are two main advantages to this, one when I am in reading mode, I can focus on topics. Second I can download a folder and create an 'ePub' or 'Mobi' file to read later on the iPad or the Kindle.

The number of articles that I clip is immense. I receive many RSS feeds and forward any articles of interest to Instapaper. From there, I do the actual reading. Having the ability to send an article to a folder, by topic, allows me to quickly organize my reading material. The end result is increased efficiency and productivity."

Michael and the Pocket app:

"I use Pocket. Augusto likes Instapaper. I've tried both and finally settled for Pocket. I find the interface easier to use. It takes less taps to share something, and I can add many articles to Pocket from the many different apps I use.

To add an article I can email it, add it from Reeder app, Tweetbot app or from Safari with a Bookmarklet.

When I want to read something, I take my iPad and just fire up the Pocket app and read the articles. They are downloaded offline so even if I'm traveling with flaky Internet connection, I can easily read everything.

When I find an article worthy of sharing with my Twitter and blog audience, I mark it with a star and share it later. When an article has content that is very relevant to my work and I'd like to keep it for later, I send it directly to Evernote to my 'Articles' notebook.

The 'read it later' apps like Instapaper or Pocket make the iPad a fantastic reading device. Again, the articles are downloaded to your iPad in a pure form, without their web sites' design - you just focus on reading."

www.youtube.com/iPadOnlyBook

Video #13: Reading later on the iPad with Pocket and Instapaper.

iPad is a perfect reader's companion

Because the iPad is a tablet device, it's much more convenient to read on it than on a laptop. The fact that you can turn it vertically and read the content in a natural way, without the keyboard, is the killer feature of the iPad. Additionally, the variety of reading apps and formats make the platform so versatile that it can appeal to any kind of reader.

File Management

Altogether, the iPad brings this paradigm shift from the files to the apps. However, to ensure compatibility with the rest of the computing world, we do have to deal with the files on the iPad. We're working with fewer files than in the past, but still a necessary evil. When we talk about 'file management', we focus on the three main applications that helped us in our #iPadOnly journey, Dropbox, Evernote and GoodReader

Dropbox

Things may change and evolve as is everything with technology, but as we wrote this book, Dropbox it is the gold standard for private file sharing and storage.

One of the main strengths of Dropbox for an #iPadOnly user, is that many apps use Dropbox as their 'syncing' mechanism. Particularly the apps that have their Android, Mac or PC counterparts. That's what makes Dropbox one of the primary tools to going #iPadOnly. Many apps prefer to sync via Dropbox rather than iCloud. This provides a more universal approach to accessing the information.

Michael on DropBox

"When I create files (or retrieve files others send to me), I store them in my Dropbox. I'm paying for additional storage as I want every file I touch to end up in Dropbox.

When a file is in Dropbox, it's not only available on any device I own (my Mac, iPhone and the Android phone I use to test Nozbe) but I can also easily share it with anyone. I simply click on the file, click to share and send a unique email link to the recipient. It's easier than sending attachments, which may be heavy (i.e. occupy lots of MBs of space). In this way, each file sent from Dropbox is a short email with a link for the recipient to view the file in the browser and optionally download if needed.

I do like the fact that you can 'star' a file to make it viewable and accessible offline but I'd also like the ability to download an entire folder for offline access. I hope that's a future feature to Dropbox."

Augusto on DropBox

Without Dropbox I would not be able to work #iPadOnly. I write in text files that are stored on Dropbox and from there many apps have access to these files (Scrivener on the Mac, for example).

I also use Dropbox to pull photos from my iPad and iPhone as an additional measure of backup until I can sync the pictures with iPhoto on my Mac."

Final Comments on Dropbox

Apple may produce a better solution, but iCloud is not quite there. Dropbox remains the gold standard for syncing. The original text of this book was also on Dropbox. We wrote in text files using the Byword app, then synced to a common folder we shared on Dropbox.

Evernote

Evernote calls itself 'your digital brain' and we must admit it feels like it's our additional brain, too. Evernote has grown to be an application that many people love and that can do as much or as little as you wish.

Michael on Evernote

"Thanks to Evernote I've cleaned up my act! Instead of writing something in a Word document or a text note and saving it as a file, I write it as an Evernote note. Luckily for me, I started using Evernote extensively 2 years prior to switching to the iPad so when I did switch, I had most of my notes already in Evernote. Now, thanks to the iPad, I use it even more.

Two features of Evernote I use extensively on the iPad are 'the email gateway' and 'offline notebooks'.

Thanks to my personal, individual Evernote email address, I can send emails directly to Evernote where they are converted to notes. This way, when I'm processing my email on the iPad, I often just forward it to Evernote. On my laptop, I'd fire up Evernote and create a note in a separate window. Thanks to the limitation of 'one window at a time' on the iPad, I learned to use the email gateway. Fast. Clean. Efficient.

Evernote is a free service but you can upgrade to 'Premium Account'. When you do, you can have notebooks in the Evernote app work offline - meaning - you can access easily all of the notes in these notebooks when your Internet connection is flaky or non-existent. I have several notebooks marked for 'offline' viewing - especially the ones with my documents scanned - this way I can access them anytime I want.

There are lots of apps that sync with Evernote and send data to Evernote. I explore these in the future chapters of this book. I'm sending articles, scans, photos, notes, sketches and many other things from many other apps directly to Evernote. Works like magic and makes Evernote my real external brain on the iPad and my central information hub."

Augusto on Evernote

"Evernote is one of those apps that has been part of my iPad since the early days. I don't consider myself an Evernote power user. I have played with it many times, but I have never been able to use it for more than a file cabinet.

On my journey to work via iPadOnly, I scan documents and send them to Evernote. I love that Evernote adds OCR technology onto documents, thus making even photos searchable.

Again, Evernote is my digital file cabinet. I don't want to use a physical file cabinet. I use the iPad and the iPhone to scan all the documents I can and send them to Evernote.

That said, I also scan most of my reference material and send it to Evernote (unless I receive them by email in which case I email directly to Evernote). This includes all of my tax related documents. I scan and send to Evernote and file the originals. When the time comes to do my taxes for the year I can simply email the notebook to my accountant and she will take care of the rest. She rarely needs the actual paper copy. The scan is simply enough."

Final Notes on Evernote

Evernote is a very powerful application that can do as much or as little as you need. Even though they offer a free version, the 'Premium' version is worth much more than the annual subscription. It is one of those interesting applications that can do almost as much as you need or as little as you want. There are people like Brett Kelly (the author of the 'Evernote Essentials' ebook) that produced an incredible amount of information on how to get the most out of Evernote, but many of those tricks are beyond the scope of this book.

Michael on GoodReader

"First off, almost every item you open in almost every app has "Open in Good Reader" option. When you do that, the file is being copied to Good Reader and now you can do whatever you want with it. You can view it, annotate it and save it... or just copy somewhere else. Save to your Dropbox? No problem. Upload to your FTP server? No biggie. Rename it? Move it?... Good Reader does it all.

Sometimes I need to send a file to someone, upload it to Dropbox, upload it to our secure server, FTP... and GoodReader does all that and more. I'd call the Good Reader app the central "file management" hub on my iPad and even though I try NOT to manage too many files on my iPad, this app makes the transition from a PC to a post-PC, #iPadOnly world, a lot easier.

Augusto on GoodReader

"Working and annotating PDF's is one of the things that I love about the iPad. It works great and is so easy. Annotate, fill, save it, email it, send it to Dropbox and much more.

You can also send your PDFs to iBooks or the Kindle application but you can't do anything other than read in these applications. With GoodReader you can do so much more.

I use less than 10% of the capability of the application, but I love to be able to annotate, sign, fill forms, email or fax them. This makes GoodReader a key application for me.

Actually, before this book was ready I worked on the file and sent it as a PDF to my iPad and made a lot of annotations using GoodReader. It really helped me get the book ready."

File Management and the #iPadOnly

Just like we discovered during our #iPadOnly work that we

didn't use the keyboard as often as we used to, we also realized that we reduced our file management when working on the iPad. In the post-PC world, the #iPadOnly world, files are less and less important as the apps themselves are being used as a means to store information. However, the above mentioned apps help make the transition smooth and ensure that we maintain compatibility with the more traditional computing world.

www.youtube.com/iPadOnlyBook

Video #14: Why Evernote and GoodReader are so helpful when working on the iPad.

Note taking

As mentioned in the 'File Management' section of this book, all of our notes end up in Evernote. This is our central hub for notes and files and paperless office.

Along with a stylus, the iPad makes a fantastic note-taking device.

We tested several styluses and note-taking apps on the iPad and finally settled on the apps described below.

Augusto uses Drafts app:

"This is the super app. It looks like a simple blank page. It opens fast and allows me to write notes from conversations. From there I can move to any other platform or email or text. My handwriting is abysmal. This application allows me to take notes during meetings and from there, process them to other platforms."

Michael likes the Moleskine Notebook app

"I take all of my hand-written notes in the Moleskine app. It has a great note taking app with several useful features like zooming and wrist-pad. It makes note-taking on the iPad easy. Whenever I'm on a call with someone I open this app and start taking notes. Later, I send each note to Evernote for further processing. The Moleskine notebook, together with the Cosmonaut stylus, is a perfect substitute for the ballpoint-pen and paper."

Michael also uses Paper app:

"I use this app more for drawing than for note-taking. I've drawn illustrations for my blog posts and this book, I draw user interfaces for my Nozbe apps and I sketch out other ideas. The app is beautiful, with only a few options and a limited toolset... but the results are stunning. I really love it. I save my finished sketches to the Camera Roll and later export them to Evernote or Dropbox or wherever I want."

www.youtube.com/iPadOnlyBook

Video #15: Paper by 53 - unleash the artist within by drawing on the iPad.

Michael is also a big fan of the Skitch app

'Skitch is an app from Evernote that I use for quick feedback loops with my programming and design teams. It's great for pointing out things to change, improve and re-design.

When they send me a link or a mockup, I press the 'home' and 'off' buttons on my iPad to catch a screenshot. Then I open the screenshot in Skitch, add a few arrows, colors, boxes, pieces of texts... what have you. Next, I export it to Camera Roll and email it back to my team or upload it to the appropriate Nozbe project or task.

It's a fantastic little app that lets me send visual feedback to my team quickly. As an added bonus, all the 'skitches' are synced with my Evernote account so I can't lose anything."

Styluses

Although you can take notes using just your fingertip, drawing on the iPad with a stylus feels more natural. You can't go wrong with any stylus and there are lots of them on the market. We recommend Bamboo as a traditional stylus and the Cosmonaut for the thicker marker-like look.

Note taking is fun on the iPad

Not only is note-taking with a stylus very natural on the iPad but it's also something that can't be done on a traditional laptop or PC. And it's so much fun. Interacting with the content, drawing, annotating, sketching... it's simply amazing.

Office Type of Applications

Let's talk about the king of the jungle, the Microsoft Office productivity suite. Word, Excel and PowerPoint are three of the most used applications for the majority of the computers users. There was a time when people would buy a computer only to be able to use Microsoft's productivity suite. In the 90's and the first decade of the 2000's this was a standard... and to some extent it still is.

However, things started to change just a few short years ago. On the PC platform OpenOffice (aka 'LibreOffice') became the new alternative. Google began making waves with their Docs & Spreadsheets package (now known as Google Drive) and Apple launched their own suite called iWork. Now, let's examine how (and if) you can do real 'office work' on the iPad and which apps have been helping us get this job done.

Apple iWork

To prove that you can 'do office work' on the iPad, Apple ported their productivity suite 'iWork' to the iOS with its three flagship apps: Pages, Numbers and Keynote. They did a very good job with these apps, focusing on taking advantage of the touch screen and making creating documents on the iPad a breeze. When they introduced iCloud support, working with these apps became easy and seamless as our documents synced with our other devices (like the iPhone or the Mac) automatically.

Keynote

Keynote is the Apple's counterpart to Microsoft's PowerPoint. However, the only thing these apps have in common is the fact that they both create presentations. Other than that, they are completely different. The late Steve Jobs was one of the masters of public speaking and he always gave stunning presentations introducing Apple's newest products. They say that the Keynote app was designed closely with Steve.

Here's what Michael thinks about Keynote

"As a new public speaker I fell in love with the original Keynote app on the Mac. All of the presentations I did in the past 5 years were done in Keynote. I know some friends who moved to Mac just because of this app. It helps create stunning presentations. It's very intuitive and extremely easy to use. And its iPad counterpart is even better. Apple took the essence of Keynote and put it on the iPad.

Now, thanks to VGA-to-iPad and HDMI-to-iPad adapters I can plug the iPad directly to a projector screen and give the presentation entirely on the iPad.

But there is more. Thanks to the iCloud, I have moved all of my past presentations there and can access and edit them directly on the iPad. Clean. Fast. Efficient. I recently had to give a speech about a subject I already assembled into a presentation. I quickly duplicated it on my iPad. With a few taps I reorganized and updated the slides, and I was on my way. And changing the slides by swiping totally rocks."

Here's Augusto's take on Keynote

"I made my living years ago doing presentations. As a Sales Manager, when you are not presenting to clients, you are training people. I use to spend hours on PowerPoint and later on Keynote for Mac. Keynote for the iPad may not be the most powerful tool available but it is good enough for most people's needs. The reality is that unless you are trying to give a very complex presentation (and in my opinion you should avoid that), Keynote on the iPad does the job.

I am a true believer that the simpler the presentation the more power it conveys. There is nothing worse than presentations that are overloaded with text and animations. They quickly distract you from the point of the speech. This is where Keynote on the iPad shines. You get enough power to build a complete, sleek-looking presentation, but not so much to over-complicate the message."

Pages

Pages is Apple's version of Word. Pages on the iPad works great for official documents, letters and the like. In our past Mac-oriented life we had several well formatted Pages documents. We put them all in the iCloud and we can now access them easily on the iPad. Most people's needs are really covered here as Pages also allows you to print directly from the iPad (if you have a compatible printer), open a document in another application, as well as share it in a Pages, PDF or Word format. Finally, you can set Pages to check spelling, word count and to display center, edge and spacing guides for when you are inserting Media, Tables, Charts or Shapes. Apple recently brought back the feature to 'track changes', making this app complete.

As we mentioned, Pages is a very powerful app, and for most people it'll be the go-to app for rich-formatted text document creation. However, from our experience you don't really need a word processor like Pages to create nice looking formatted text. You can simply open Evernote and write a note. The basic options of fonts, bold, italics and the like are there. Or you can open Byword and write a pure text file with Markdown formatting and export or print the formatted document. Believe it or not, there are many ways to create a rich-formatted document on the iPad.

Numbers

Numbers is Apple's version of Excel and we'd say it's the 'sexy' Excel. It's easier to use, the spreadsheets look great and there are several trendy designs to choose from.

Michael on Numbers

"I keep my company's critical statistical data in Numbers. Again, as with the other iWork apps, I imported all my past Numbers documents to the iCloud so I could access and edit them on the iPad easily."

Augusto on Numbers

"I am an advanced user of Excel on a PC, but my current work doesn't require that I use macros, or anything more complicated than formulas and graphs. My spreadsheets are not as complex as they were in the past. This allows me to use and enjoy them on the iPhone and the iPad. Unless you have a need for advanced Excel features (for example Macros and Pivot Tables), the iPad's Numbers app has adequate horse power. I have a long history of using it as my main software to access, create and edit Excel sheets without any issue."

Google Drive - formerly known as Docs and Spreadsheets.

Google is offering fantastic apps for free in exchange for all the information we can give them. This is spooky on one hand... and dangerous on the other. Historically, Google is known for 'just trying' some services and then shutting them down if they didn't get enough traction or are simply not aligned with the current corporate policy of Google. This is what recently happened to one of our favorite web apps - GoogleReader.

During our quest of going #iPadOnly we've been trying to avoid Google's services as much as possible, but there are two we simply couldn't dodge completely. Google Drive and Gmail. Most importantly, the 'Docs and Spreadsheets' features within Google Drive.

When you're collaborating with others, the Google Drive app is the only way to do real-time collaboration. When you open a document, you can see if someone else is browsing the document, editing it... you can actually see where their cursor is at that very moment.

It all sounds really great...

We tried to use Google Drive to co-write this book. Unfortunately, we failed. Initially we thought of putting everything on Google Drive directly - to write the chapters in Google Drive.

However, we both prefer to use Byword to write text - it's fast, has a great full screen mode and you can change the background to black and text to white... and it's really fast to work with. So, we'd type the chapter in Byword and later copy and paste it to Google Drive. After we wrote the first chapter and started writing the second one, we realized this method was inefficient. During phase one of writing the book it was an overkill to use Google Drive. We switched back to Dropbox - shared a folder together and focused on writing in Byword. Later in the process, we decided to work with Google Drive once we'd start editing entire chapters together in real-time.

Then the editing part of the process arrived and we realized we still didn't like how Google Drive operated. It was slow when writing and editing; it was even slower when opening the files. It just wasn't efficient to use. We decided to keep working in Byword with Dropbox on the backend. We solved the 'real time collaboration' problem by putting tasks in Nozbe. When someone would edit Chapter 1, they'd put it as a task and the other one knew they were not to touch it until the other one finished. It worked great for us.

In the end, we still recommend Google Drive for ad-hoc document collaboration and sharing, but not for serious book writing or editing. It's too slow and too clumsy for projects of this extent.

www.youtube.com/iPadOnlyBook

Video #16: Google Drive no more - our struggle editing the book on the iPad.

Working with "real" Microsoft Office files

Contrary to popular opinion, you can work on DOC (docx), XLS (xlsx) or PPT (pptx) files directly on the iPad. And there are several apps for that.

Augusto uses Office2HD

"This is my choice when I work with Word documents. It is an application that allows me to do everything that I need so I come back to this application often. In my experience, this application can do everything that Pages can, but it adds two important features - the ability to 'track changes' and to access the Cloud.

I rely heavily on 'track changes'. Between other writers and editors it is very important to be able to see their work. For a long time, this was something that constantly drove me back to the MacBook and it was frustrating. I can now work directly on the iPad and see the changes. This allows me to easily accept or reject them.

The second reason I prefer Office2HD over Pages is the integration with the Cloud. I rely on Dropbox for many things and on Google Drive for those projects that I am working on with other people or simply that I am collaborating. Since this application allows me to directly connect to Dropbox, GoogleDrive, SkyDrive, Box.net and more, it makes my job easy. No need to email documents."

Michael uses QuickOffice HD

""When I moved to the #iPadOnly world I decided to gradually change my workflows and to revise the apps I need for day-to-day work. I no longer use Word and Excel files on a daily basis, but continue to have the occasional need.

There are several apps that assist Microsoft Office on the iPad and one of them is QuickOffice HD. The developers behind this app have moved on to Google (the Silicon Valley giant actually bought their company) so I don't know how long this app will be supported. For now it works and does the job.
I save all of the past DOC and XLS files in Dropbox. I then access them directly through Dropbox with this app. When I need to update an Excel sheet or a Word document, I can do it right there.

For example, I have an Excel file I need to update weekly. This app serves this purpose well."

www.youtube.com/iPadOnlyBook

Video #17: Microsoft Office on the iPad - apps that get the job done.

You can do office work on the iPad

The iPad is now a mature platform with many apps that effectively assist with 'office work' You can use Apple's iWork suite, you can work on Microsoft's Office files (without any help from Microsoft, actually) and so much more. You simply can be an #iPadOnly office kind of person if you want to, although we believe that Microsoft's productivity suite will be losing relevance in the #iPadOnly world.

Email

Email is a necessary evil. You may like it or not. You may process it or not. You can run from it, but you cannot hide. Many people run and hope that it never catches up with them, but it always does.

Augusto on Email

"I have been reading and processing email on a mobile phone for a long time, going back to the day when I got my Palm Treo. When I got my first iPhone I considered that an improvement over how my old Treo had handled email. Next, I was honestly surprised how nice it was to process email on the iPad. When I went #iPadOnly, I also re-formatted my MacBook. When that happened I decided to only install and configure things as needed. I found I never needed to configure email on my MacBook. I process all email from the iPad."

Michael on Email

"The notion that you could 'touch your email' was very appealing to me when I got my first iPhone; even more so with the iPad. Honestly, I wasn't convinced the built-in Mail application would be sufficient for the daily email workload, but it was."

Email is tough

Working with email it is a matter of workflow. If you are resisting email, you may need to study your email workflow and see how you can improve it. We don't love email, but we have come to like working with email on the iPad over the Mac or the iPhone without any doubt.

Augusto turned off email completely on his iPhone. He realized that email on his phone was more of a distraction, and now he processes it only on the iPad.

We both use the standard, built-in Mail app on the iPad. It gets the job done, is decent and fast. We both use Gmail for email. It has a great spam filter and a fantastic web app when you're using it on the desktop. We take advantage of the Gmail's support of the IMAP protocol to configure it with the native Apple's Mail application.

How to find an email

There is only one reason we have the native Gmail application installed on the iPad. Search. If you are in Gmail you can use it whenever you want to find an email message from the past. We are aware that the Mail app also has a search feature, but it's slow and cumbersome due to the limitations of the IMAP protocol, whereas the search in the Gmail app is almost instantaneous. It is not every day that we need to search for past emails, but it is worth it to have that app. The time it saves you is enough to recommend installing it.

www.youtube.com/iPadOnlyBook

Video #18: Dealing with email on the iPad - inbox zero thanks to the apps.

Michael and the Multiple "from" addresses trick

"Although the iPad's settings let you set up your Gmail account automatically, I didn't choose this option. Instead, I set up my email through IMAP. It's a little more complicated to set up as you need to input the addresses of the IMAP server (imap.gmail.com) and SMTP server (smtp.gmail.com) but it gives you a cool trick - you can set up several 'from fields'. If you have several 'from' addresses set up in Gmail, you can use them all directly in Apple's mail when you add them to your 'from' field in Settings. Here's what my 'From' field looks like in my Settings: 'michael@sliwinski.com, michael@nozbe.com'. Now, if I get an email to my Nozbe address and I want to reply to it, it'd be automatically replied from this address. The same rule applies to my private address. It's a trick, but it works. If I compose a new message I can use a drop-down list to choose which email address I want to appear on my sent email."

Horizontal view and vertical view

Once again, we'd like to highlight the versatility of the horizontal and vertical views. We both process email with the iPad set horizontally (Landscape mode), with the list of emails on the left and the current email message on the right. When we want to focus on an email message, we simply flip the iPad vertically (Portrait mode) and read the message without any distractions. It is this kind flexibility that can't be replicated on the laptop.

More on email from Michael

"For email processing in horizontal mode, I rarely have my external keyboard attached. I use the iPad with the smart cover to support it. I'm accustomed to writing short replies so I simply tap them away on the on-screen keyboard. When I have a few longer emails to write I put my iPad in vertical mode docked in the Logitech's Ultrathin keyboard and focus on writing. Again, processing on the iPad makes working through email so much fun."

More on email from Augusto

"I rarely process email from my desk. Most of the time, I move to a couch or other comfortable place. I type fast enough on the onscreen keyboard that if I have a short answer I can type it there. If the email requires a longer reply, I'll wait until I finish processing the rest of my emails and then process it from my desk. I read email in landscape mode. I only check email if I think I can read and process them all. I try to avoid just reading email, it is the reason I have email on the iPhone turned off. I discovered that on the iPhone I was mostly 'checking' but it is on the iPad that I was 'processing' email."

Email "gateways"

As we mentioned in earlier chapters, many apps like Evernote, TripIt, Pocket, Instapaper, Nozbe and others, assign you an individual email address for use within each app. This allows you to add these 'app email addresses' as contacts to your iPad and later forward the appropriate emails to the appropriate app (notes to Evernote, tasks to Nozbe, airline tickets to TripIt, articles to Pocket, etc.). This seemingly small tip will have a remarkable effect on your iPad productivity..

More Email apps

There are many new email apps available to the iPhone and the iPad. These more focused apps allow us, *finally,* to improve our 'email processing workflow' and get to the mystical 'Inbox Zero'.

Apps like Mailbox, Triage and others help us manage email and develop good habits. Over at Nozbe, Michael's team is working on a new email app called 'Emailine' to be announced in the summer of 2013. It will be tightly integrated with Michael's Nozbe task and project management system. Michael believes that you can't have a great task management system without a great email app to go with it that makes email messages 'actionable' items.

This last paragraph was by no means an ad for these products. All we want to point out is that what gets us excited with the iOS platform and the #iPadOnly way, is that there truly always is 'an app for that' and that better email apps are just round the corner and will appear on the platform very soon.

Suffice to say, the iPad is a very powerful, versatile email machine and enables you to really 'touch your email'.

Communication

When the iPad was announced the amount of jokes on the web regarding the fact that the iPad looks like a giant phone were readily abundant. Although the iPad is not a giant phone by design, it can be, at least in the sense that it can actually be a very capable communication device.

It all starts with the two built-in communication features of the iPad - iMessage and FaceTime. However, they are not the only ones. You can also use other communication giants' apps like Skype, Facebook Messenger or most recently, Google Hangouts. You can also try lesser known tools, designed for more specific needs, like Yammer, Socialcast, Hipchat or others.

iMessage

iMessage is basically a free text messaging tool between iOS and Macs.

When Apple introduced iMessage and the ability to start a message on the iPhone, then continue it on the iPad and then jump to the Mac, they were onto something great. The best part is that Apple made it completely seamless. You'd send a text message (SMS) to someone and whether they had an iPhone or iPad or Mac, they'd receive it. And it'd cost you nothing to send the iMessage. It's something truly magical. Especially for all those that are constantly sending texts (SMS) to people in other countries.

Augusto on iMessage

"Apple is competing very well with WhatsApp which is in my

opinion the king of multi-platform text message. I do business with people in Latin America and the US, and have friends in Europe. Not everyone has 'iDevices', so being able to communicate with them through free text and image messaging via WhatsApp is incredible. However, I noticed that people with iPhones and iPads tend to prefer iMessage over WhatsApp (which is not available for the iPad), and the reason is simple: there is something really wonderful to be able to begin a conversation on one machine and continue on the other, giving you a real flexibility and the speed that many need to be able to really keep a text conversation while moving along in their day."

Michael remembers his first iMessage well

"I was sending a usual 'text SMS message' with my iPhone to a friend in a different country and the message got sent as a 'blue' message instead of the usual 'green' one. What it meant was that it got sent through the Internet for free as an iMessage to the recipient without either of us having to sign up for anything. It was a great experience. That's why I was happy when iMessage also became available on the iPad and the Mac. It's not only registered with my cellular phone number but also with my email address. It works great. When I need to send a short message to someone and I want this message to reach them immediately, I don't write an email but I start an iMessage conversation and choose their email address. When the address turns blue, I know they have an iMessage account and what I'm about to send them gets to their mobile device right away. Clean. Fast. Efficient

The cool thing is that the recipient doesn't have to own an iPhone to have an iMessage account. They can also have an iPad or a Mac. Or both. Or all three of them. It just works."

FaceTime

The natural extension of iMessage is FaceTime. It works where iMessage works and is the 'voice and video' version of the service. Again, members of the Nozbe team often have the need to call and discuss something. Augusto also uses it for business as well as for pleasure. Augusto's parents and in-laws live far away and they love to tell stories to their grandkids via FaceTime. It compensates for the distance and assures that the grandparents are not strangers to the kids.

There is something nice in being able to see each other's faces - since we all work from home, it's a nice bonus. While writing this book, we'd hold regular 'Weekly Review' sessions with each other via FaceTime. Being on two different continents, yet video chatting as if we were in the same room, feels great every time.

Whatsapp

This app is still the 'king of multi-platform messaging' but it's actually not available for the iPad. We write about it as we use it on our iPhones and we both think it's a mistake WhatsApp doesn't offer an iPad version. It could be authenticated with your phone number. This would really give iMessage a run for its money and most of all, would allow us to communicate to all of our friends and peers who prefer the other (Android) platform. Apart from being available on our operating systems, the other great thing about WhatsApp is the fact that it compresses both photos and videos upon sending so it makes even the multimedia messages almost instantaneous. Well, time will tell if they make the move to the iPad.

Skype

Skype is still the most popular way to communicate if you want to chat, talk or video-talk and we both use it every day. It's available on all of the platforms, including Android and PC (unlike iMessage and FaceTime). Skype was the first company that brought video-conferencing to the masses.

When the calls and chats with friends and teammates can't be done using iMessage or FaceTime we use Skype and it works great. The iPad client has improved substantially over the last years. However, you're still unable to record conversations or video conversations. We recorded a series of video chats for this book and we had to use a Mac for that... and we shouldn't need to.

The great thing about Skype that's still not possible on FaceTime is the feature that allows group calling. Simply put. you can call a group of people and talk with all of them at once on Skype. OK, when you're on the iPad, you can join the conversation but you can't start one. Again, Michael, who is doing lots of group chats, is hoping this feature is coming to the iPad's Skype client sooner rather than later.

Socialcast

This is the Nozbe team's 'private' social network. This is where the company chats. If you know what IRC was (and still is), it's something similar, just from this century. Everyone in the company has a Socialcast account and they chat about things both related and unrelated to the company and work. It's like a water cooler in a remote office - people meet there and chat. Throughout each day messages, links and photos show up that folks want to share with the rest of the Nozbe team.

Michael's opinion

"I know companies that prefer to do a 'private Facebook' group for social chatting in the company but we chose not to. This would mean we'd have to go to the Facebook app (or web site) to chat - once there, it'd be very tempting to keep on browsing our Facebook timeline. That's why we chose to separate our own social network. We want to chat with our team and then get back to work."

HipChat

Socialcast is nice but Nozbe's developers needed a real-time chat for their work and they decided to use Hipchat. They love it. Now they feel like they are in the same 'office' as they can chat in real time and exchange ideas. What's more, Hipchat integrates with their development tools like GitHub. Every piece of code sent to GitHub now gets pushed to Hipchat - this way Nozbe developers 'communicate through code'. They are currently working on a Nozbe/Hipchat integration to push comments in 'Nozbe development' projects to Hipchat as well. That's their missing link.

Google Hangouts

This is the new kid on the block. Google has been trying to get into the social media arena and the Hangouts are their latest version to try to conquer that arena. Sadly, it is neither user friendly or fail-proof, making it hard to win people over from Skype and FaceTime. In our testing, Google Hangouts worked well with decent video and very good audio quality, but it crashed too often during our conversations, which was very annoying. Hopefully Google will fix it soon.

The iPad is a great communication device

It's not a bigger iPhone but it really can be. You can talk to people, video-chat with them and exchange messages easily. There are apps from the big players as well as from the niche ones and they all help us stay in touch together. If you use Skype-out service you can even call 'normal phones' right from the iPad. We both enjoy staying in touch with people through the iPads and barely miss a beat from the desktop apps. We both use iPad for communication in business as well as our private lives and it does more than enough to cover our needs.

Social Media

We are both quite active in Social Media. And being active in Social Media with an iPad at hand is fun. So much fun in fact that we both have to 'schedule' our social media time to make sure we don't spend too much time 'connecting' with our friends on all of the available platforms.

iPad is the Social Media hub

Social Media is one of the great reasons for going #iPadOnly. Apps offered by the major networks are simply better and more fun to interact with on the iPad than from their web sites. With the iPad in hand, it's easy and more engaging. This is why we do all of our Social Media activities on the iPad.

The integration helps

The bonus feature of the iOS is its integration with both Twitter and Facebook. You can add your social media accounts to the iPad and basically share anything on these networks. We use this to tweet out our thoughts by sharing photos and links.

Twitter

Michael is Tweeting from his iPad:

"Most of the time, I use the official Twitter client on the iPad - especially when I want to browse my 'Connect' tab. This is where I see who's replying to me, who's re-tweeting and favoring my tweets and who just started following me.

For casual Twitter browsing and more interaction with the

platform I still prefer the Tweetbot client. For a few reasons:

- gestures - swiping, tapping, double-tapping and other gestures help me interact with the timeline more efficiently

- timeline based on lists - I can switch from my 'general' timeline to the lists I created. Very cool if I want to browse tweets from just a handful of the people I'm following (like all the productivity gurus, startup founders, etc...)

- integration with Pocket and/or Instapaper - when someone tweets a link, I usually quickly 'preview' it and if it feels like an interesting article, I move it to my Pocket and read it later.

So there you have it - I use the official Twitter client for replying and interacting with people and the Tweetbot client to browse my timeline."

Augusto decided not to tweet from his iPad:

"I don't do Twitter on the iPad. As you will discover later in this chapter, I only use HootSuite when I participate in Twitter chats, because I think it's the best solution. HootSuite and the use of columns really make chatting great. I know people who use the iPhone, the MacBook and the iPad in order to be active on the Twitter chats, but I have discovered that by having HootSuite set up correctly, it is more than enough. The rest of my Twitter activity happens on the iPhone."

HootSuite

HootSuite it is one of those applications that try to do many things at once. It wants to be your Social Media Hub. As mentioned above, Augusto is using it for Twitter chatting:

"I have a column for each Twitter Chat. One for 'Mentions' and one for 'Direct Messages'. Using columns allow me to actively keep up with the speed and volume that these chats tend to have. Again, at least for the iPad, I have not found a better solution than this"

Michael uses HootSuite for "Social Media monitoring":

"I use HootSuite to do more advanced searches than the standard Twitter app allows. I have columns set up to display ho mentions 'Nozbe', who mentions me, our book, our hashtag (#iPadOnly) etc. By browsing the column I can see what's happening in the areas of my interest."

Facebook

Facebook it the elephant in the 'social media' room. This is how we use it on the iPad:

Michael and Facebook:

"I use the official Facebook clients - the 'Facebook' app and the 'Pages' app. I don't use the 'Messages' app as I prefer not to communicate through Facebook. I have my email Inbox and I prefer to have conversations there. Sometimes people do send me messages via Facebook, but I just reply to these through the Facebook app and that's it.

As I manage (or help manage) Nozbe's Facebook page, my official page and other pages, I use the 'Pages' app. If you're into Facebook, interacting with it on the iPad is nice and fast. I don't remember when I last opened the Facebook web site - I access it only from the iPad app."

c

Augusto and Facebook:

"I mostly use the Facebook Pages app. I maintain 'Augusto Pinaud Books' as well as my productivity podcast in Spanish

'Productivo en 25 Minutos'. I use this application to access and see what's happening there. I prefer to have one application only, mostly because I don't see the advantage of a second application and for keeping them separate."

Linkedin

The 'professional social site' finally has a very mature and fast iPad app.

Michael's take on LinkedIn:

"As I'm not looking for a job (I love my current job as the founder and CEO of Nozbe, thank you very much), I'm not using the site very extensively but I do accept invitations and connect with busy professionals from all over the world. With this app it's very easy to do so."

Augusto prefers the LinkedIn web site:

"Their iPhone App it is a little basic but it's getting better with each update. On the iPad the story changes, because I can access LinkedIn in the browser to have the real experience. This is where I choose to act and join that particular network. I am not as active as I should be but I want to use it more."

Pinterest

Michael is using Pinterest to post his sketches:

"I'm not as active on Pinterest as I'd like to be but I still use it occasionally. Their iPad app is very nice and works extremely fast. And you can 'pin' anything by adding their Bookmarklet to your Safari's bookmarks. I use it mainly to post my sketches done with the Paper app."

Google+

Google+ is still a mixed bag for both of us. We think their app is very pretty, but we still don't 'get' the social media effort of Google.

Michael on Google+:

"Some people swear by it. Others hate it. I'm still undecided. I don't like the fact that you can't post or interact with the site from anywhere else other than their official site or app. No API, no external integrations. That said, their iPad app is very pretty and if you're into this network, you'll love the iPad experience."

Augusto on Google+:

"Google pushed people to join their platform Google Plus and they have killed many things to push people to get there. Most recently they killed Google Reader in order to convince people to share more stuff using Google Plus. My personal opinion is that it feels more like Google *Push* than Google Plus. I like the speed of Twitter, I understand the idea behind Facebook, but honestly, I never really understood what Google Plus is all about. I don't know if it is in part that Google is pushing us toward there and I have a natural tendency to go against authority, or the fact that I see it as a black hole. It does so much that I am not totally sure it does anything really well. I am expecting that soon Google will kill Google Groups in an effort to push more people into using Google Plus. I am not sure that even that will encourage me to use it more."

Buffer

We both love Buffer. It's a great little app that allows you to schedule your Social Media posts to make sure you don't overwhelm your followers with too many messages at once. We both use it mainly for Twitter but you can also set it up with Facebook or LinkedIn. It is very easy to use and you can send data and links directly for many applications like Instapaper, Pocket, Drafts, Email and more.

Social Media apps rock the iPad

The great thing about the iPad and the entire iOS platform is the 'appification' of the Internet. We mentioned this in the chapter about 'Web Browsing'. The situation here is similar. On a 'normal PC' you'd have to go to the Facebook web site, LinkedIn site and other sites, even though some apps for these platforms exist. On the iPad, you'd practically never visit the sites, as the apps are so much better. They have a more natural and engaging feel with the social media networks. The respective companies double-down on their app development and these apps are getting better day by day. This is why we can't imagine *NOT* doing social media on the iPad - it adds to our last chapter's argument that the iPad is a very powerful communications device.

www.youtube.com/iPadOnlyBook

Video #19: Social Media on the iPad - Twitter, Facebook, Pinterest and more...

Writing.

The 'plain text format' is back! After years of using Microsoft Word and other 'rich text' apps and fiddling with bold, italics, styles, font sizes and the like... we're finally back with writing in simple text. This seems like a step back, but in reality, it's an improvement. It helps us to focus on just writing and not playing with formatting.

Yes, you can still write formatted text in many apps on the iPad. But the 'plain text' format (especially with Markdown styling) makes the process easier and most of all, distraction-free.

Michael on writing in plain text:

"All of the chapters of this book, all of my blog posts - everything starts in plain text format. I use a Markdown format which is a way of writing text that adds formatting by just writing **bold** or *italics* instead of playing with the B and I buttons in the button bar. It sounds a little 'geeky' but it's actually very effective once you get the hang of it (more on Markdown a little further in this chapter).

As my co-author, Augusto, puts it - when you write in simple plain text format, your only option is to write or not to write, you don't waste time fiddling with other options. He's so right about this one."

Augusto has written several books like that already:

"I like working in plain text files that sync with my Dropbox and can later be picked up by Scrivener to put the book together when I jump over to the Mac. We've been co-writing this book the same way. Both of us writing text files and syncing with a shared Dropbox folder. It's easy and effective. I am hoping that Michael and I will write the second edition of this book after iOS 7 ships and another book that I hope he will accept. Suffice to say, the 'text files in Dropbox' process works for both myself and for co-writing a book with someone else."

Now that we explained how we love text files, let's jump to a detailed description of why the iPad is a writer's best friend and in our opinion, the best tool around. Along the way, let's talk about some apps as well.

Byword

This is Augusto's app of choice and an app he recommended to Michael when they started working on this project. Now that Michael switched to Byword and explained to Augusto how the Markdown formatting works, Augusto is even more confident with his app choice. Augusto writes with black background and white text.

Michael switched from Nebulous Notes to Byword:

"When I started writing this book I was using an app called Nebulous - I liked it a lot - it syncs with Dropbox and has a very nice full-screen mode. When I started talking to Augusto about this book, he mentioned he was using a different app called Byword. It didn't take long for me to make the switch. Byword is more beautiful, better designed and most of all syncs with both iCloud and Dropbox perfectly. It also supports Markdown brilliantly.

Most importantly - it doesn't have a button bar - I can type on a full screen without any distractions. All I can see is text on my iPad.

The best part - I use the Logitech Ultrathin Keyboard and while the default orientation of the iPad there is horizontal, I can easily put the iPad in the vertical orientation. This is a game-changer for me - you can't do this with any laptop. My iPad is black, when it 'stands' in vertical orientation in front of me, with my text color set to white and background to black... it's by far the best writing environment ever. The text is laid out vertically just like a traditional sheet of paper. It conveys the feeling that I'm really writing something important. Like this book.

This app, together with the Logitech's Ultrathin keyboard and the iPad set in vertical orientation, makes it the best writer's machine ever."

AI Writer

This is an app Michael was also using before he switched to Byword. He keeps the app around for two main features:

- focus mode - helps the writer maintain focus by highlighting only two lines of text in the middle.

- automatic scrolling - as you type, the text is always displayed in the middle of the screen and it scrolls up automatically as you type new sentences. This helps you stay focused on what you're writing even more.

DualMailT

Augusto found this gem of an app recently and it's the only app on the iOS App Store that allows him to see two columns of different text on the same screen.

Augusto uses this app very often to translate text:

"I do a lot of work translating text from one language to

another. This is a process that was really easy to do anywhere but on the iPad. It wasn't until I discovered DualMailT that I finally had a dual text screen to work on different texts. Previously, it required a bunch of tricks, or I'd simply pull the laptop out and finish the job.

The application is super simple; it allows you to have two text screens opened side by side. I love this for writing as well as translating. I can start with the text of one language on the left and add the translated text on the right. If I am in writing mode I put the outline on the left and write the text on the right. To this day I don't understand why there aren't more applications with this feature, especially applications that are aimed at writers, who love outlines and text on the same screen."

Textastic

This 'writing app' deserves a different chapter as it's actually not for writing text, but for writing code.

Michael occasionally continues to code and he finds Textastic to be one of the best IDEs out there:

"Being the CEO of the company doesn't give me too much time to code and every developer on my team can code faster and better than I can anyway. But sometimes, out of necessity or simple curiosity, I like to dive into code and tinker with a script or something... and I do it in Textastic.

This app features amazing code-highlighting for practically every language there is (PHP, MySQL, JavaScript, Ruby, Python... you name it) and works with any kind of connection like FTP, SFTP, Dropbox and others. It also features amazing search capabilities. This is invaluable when you're coding and you want to quickly find a line of code that interests you.

In addition, it works offline and later syncs the file to the same place as it was downloaded. It's very convenient - I download a script via SFTP from one of my servers, modify it and hit 'upload' and Textastic knows exactly where the file should be sent to. If you do any kind of coding on the iPad - this is the app to use."

Markdown format for text files

We mentioned Markdown several times in this chapter so we decided to give you a quick overview of what it actually means to write in Markdown. Once a file is written in plain text using Markdown format, it can be sent later as HTML, DOC or other text with all the formatting intact. It divides the process of writing text and of exporting/formatting text.

Markdown was invented by John Gruber of Daring Fireball blog fame. Here is a quick Markdown cheat sheet:

To add **bold** just use two asterisks, *italic* requires just one.

* a bullet point goes like this
* just start the line with asterisk

Hyperlink can be written like this: [Nozbe](http://www.nozbe.com/)

Or can be written like this: [Nozbe][n]
and defined later:
[n]: http://www.nozbe.com/

An image can be added like this:
![Nozbe logo](http://www.nozbe.com/logo.png)

It's a fantastic way of writing in plain text on the iPad while at the same time making your text formatted for the web. The best part? All of the leading text editors for the iPad (Byword, Nebulous, AI Writer, and many more) support Markdown natively and can export your formatted written text to the web, email, or even a Pages or Word document.

Here's Augusto's take on Markdown:

"Michael was bragging about Markdown since our first call, and I finally decided to check 'The Mac Sparky Markdown Field Guide' to see if I could learn it, too.

I was reluctant to use Markdown; worried it would become a distraction instead of a tool. The reality is that for certain things it is very effective for writing. I'm not even close to mastering it, but the little things I am able to do have proved useful, so I am grateful to Michael for bringing it to my attention.

Markdown converts the plain text from a simple to a formatted form in a magical way. I'm still a beginner but as it becomes more natural to me, I can tell it will become my favorite form of writing. From that moment on, regular plain text writing will be gone forever in the same way that my handwriting was forever changed by the first Palm Graffiti writing. I will never write a 'T' the same way again."

That's why if you're considering going #iPadOnly as a writer, which we totally recommend, think about getting a good text editor that lets you write in full screen and supports Markdown. Dedicate some time to learn the basics of Markdown and you will never look back.

Pages, Word, Evernote and other editors that support text formatting

If you're the kind of writer that likes text formatting in a visual way, you can still use these apps and write in any format you choose. We just believe an #iPadOnly writer is best off with a plain text format supported by Markdown formatting.

We're both writers. Augusto has already written several books and for Michael, this is his first one. We're both bloggers and we both write essays and columns for magazines. We think the iPad can be the writer's best tool in his toolbox. It's very portable, you can write in portrait mode, you have great full-screen-and-very-focused apps and writing in plain text is just brilliant. If there is a profession that can go #iPadOnly the easiest, we believe it's the writer.

Blogging

Regular blogging is really hard. It doesn't seem that hard - you write a piece of text and you post it online on a blogging platform. But that's not the whole story. If you want your posts to look good, you need to prepare good illustrations or photos. You also need to format your post, tweak your post title and after all this your blog post is finally ready for posting. But...the job doesn't stop there. You then begin the next stage of posting it to all of your social media outlets (Twitter, Facebook, LinkedIn... etc.). Let's not get started on tweaking and modifying your Wordpress blog installation. Simply stated, it's a lot of work.

Michael on Blogging

"In theory, blogging should only be about writing. This is why I really loved a blogging platform called 'Posterous'. It was easy. I'd simply write a longer email and send it to the blog - the platform would convert my email to a blog post and automatically post it to my social media outlets. I loved it. Sadly the platform didn't have a viable business model so it sold itself to Twitter and subsequently was shut down at the beginning of 2013.

Because working on my iPad forced me to focus on correct workflows, I decided to migrate from Posterous to a blogging platform that would help me simplify my blogging process.

It started with Dropbox. Dropbox has a very good API so why not use it for blogging - why not just write blog posts as text files and put them in a folder in Dropbox and they'd get posted automatically?

There are several projects like this in the works (as well as some open-source software packages, and maybe even plug-ins for Wordpress) but I asked my Nozbe developers to write a custom blog for both our Nozbe site and my blog.

Suffice to say, I now write everything in text files in the Byword app on my iPad. I format my writing in the popular format Markdown. I put each of my posts in a special 'drafts' folder and I write from there. When I have an illustration or photo, I simply upload it using the Dropbox app to another magic 'images' folder. When a post is ready, I set up a date of posting by writing it at the beginning of the post's text. A special script scans my 'drafts' and 'images' folders in Dropbox every few hours and when there is a post that needs to be posted - it gets published.

After that, another script posts information from this blog post to my social media outlets. Easy. All I have to do is write and occasionally prepare an illustration.

I realize this might not be very helpful to you, as not everyone has programmers working for them to create a system like this, but actually, because there are several similar platforms already on the Internet, it's the question of finding one and setting it up for yourself. My point in this chapter was to give you an idea of simplifying your blogging setup - of making sure you focus on what's really important. On writing. Maybe that's why Seth Godin (a very famous marketing blogger and writer, the author of 'Linchpin', 'Purple Cow' and other bestselling books) never switched from his TypePad blogging platform to anything modern? His old platform is familiar to him and makes him just focus on writing. That's why I set this up the way I did. I just fire up the Byword app and create a new text file on my Dropbox and write."

Augusto on Blogging

"This is an area that needs improvement in my current workflow. I don't have a programmer that can help me develop a better system. My posts are mostly text, and my blogs are all in Wordpress, via the Wordpress application for iOS. It is not perfect in any way, shape or form, but it can be worked with certain level of success.

Again for what I do that are mostly text, the application is good enough. I can access Stats, Create Post, Categories and even access to the dashboard and more. The only thing that I don't do in this application is work with images. For that I log into the web interface. Currently, I create most of my posts in plain text using Byword. Later, after they are finished and edited, I copy and paste into the app, set the posting date and categories and I am set. The Wordpress App makes accomplishing this work fast and simple.

www.youtube.com/iPadOnlyBook

Video #20: Blogging on the iPad - why the iPad is the blogger's best friend.

Other blogging platforms

Another good blogging platform is Tumblr (recently acquired by Yahoo) which has a great iOS app. Michael uses this app to upload short info to the Nozbe's 'test blog' and 'status blog'.

As with writing, a blogger should also feel at home on the iPad and find it a very powerful and easy-to-use tool for his blogging needs.

Journaling

Journaling is a excellent habit. Both of us are doing it regularly and, of course, we journal on our iPads:

Augusto is journaling in Day One:

"I am a believer that the process of writing a Journal helps one grow, therefore it is not a surprise that I have been journaling on my iPhone and my iPad since the first opportunity appeared. Currently the application I use is called Day One.

I really like this application for journaling. I actually like it so much than when I made the decision to use it as my permanent journaling solution, I imported everything I had in my previous app to Day One and have not looked back since.

I am a believer that Journaling helps you clarify things, identify patterns, work on stuff over time and in general covers a whole set of positive attributes."

Michael is journaling in Byword:

"Journaling provides an opportunity to pause every day to think about the day I just had and to contemplate if there is something new to learn from it, some idea I need to sketch... or anything else. It's a very hard habit to instill and sometimes I forget to journal but I always try to get back to it.

To pick up the journaling habit I started with the Day One app. But in the end I actually ditched it. I decided to simplify and do something else instead. I started journaling in my favorite text editor - Byword. Here's my workflow:

For each month I create a new file in iCloud in ByWord with the year and the month - for March of 2013 the file had a name of '2013-03'. I write in that file using Markdown. Each day starts with a header of the day of the month and the week: '# 1, Friday' and what follows are my thoughts for each day starting with bullet points. The order of the days is descending - the newest day is at the top of the file, the oldest at the bottom. Here's a sample entry:

2, Saturday
* Great weekend with my family
* Went to the movies with our 4-year old, had great fun

1, Friday
* New month, new challenges, let's get that new version of Nozbe done at last!

OK, you get the idea. Now, when the month is done I create a new file with the new month. I open the old month again, read through it, add something if need be and export it 'formatted' (again, thanks to Markdown) through email to Evernote to a special notebook with a 'journal' tag. Then I delete the file and focus on the new month.

That's it. This is how I journal. It's so easy; because I'm using the tools I know and love - Byword and Evernote."

www.youtube.com/iPadOnlyBook

Video #21: Journaling on the iPad - Day One vs simple text files.

Traveling with the iPad

Traveling

We don't want to repeat ourselves here, but all the advantages of the 'new office paradigm' and iPad's hardware design apply here, too. It's simple - iPad is the best computer to travel with - it's small, weighs 1 lb and the battery lasts for 10 hours. Traveling with such a device is bliss.

Size

The small size makes it easy to access anywhere - in the line for the customs or airport security, in the plane, even if you're traveling on a low-cost airline where the space between the seats is very limited. Its size makes the iPad a perfect device for traveling.

Battery life

On a long-haul flight across the Atlantic or the Pacific when the flight is 12-13 hours, including the time to board, eat meals and walks around the cabin, the iPad battery lasts the entire flight. Easily.

Airport security

According to American TSA regulations, you don't have to remove your iPad from your bag. In Europe they treat the iPad as a laptop and always ask to see it. Again, the iPad is so small and so handy that it's not an inconvenience.

Apps

Now we're coming to the fun part. The apps on the iPad make traveling even more enjoyable.

First, the apps we mentioned before.

We use 1Password for storing passwords to travel sites and Evernote to save all the boarding passes and confirmations. We use alternate browsers like Mercury Browser or Google Chrome to browse some travel sites as a'Mac OSX' machine (so that we don't get redirected to the 'mobile' site).

Apart from these apps, there are a few fantastic specialty apps that we use for traveling.

TripIt

Whenever we're traveling we love to use TripIt. Simply forward all your confirmation emails (flights, car rentals, hotel bookings, everything) to TripIt's email address and it takes care of the rest. It puts the trip plans in order and even adds the dates and times to your calendar. On the iPad, being able to forward an email to an app is so useful - no copying and pasting, just a quick forward and the app does the rest. (That's exactly how we forward notes to Evernote and tasks to Nozbe.)

Apart from all that magic, TripIt is a nice app that allows you to see all of your travel arrangements in one place. Very handy and very visual. TripIt works both on the iPhone and the iPad and both apps sync with your TripIt account.

FlightTrackPro and FlightRadar24

When it comes to flying, it feels like magic that you can now track flights in real time.. Apps like FlightTrackPro or FlightRadar24 give a real-time view on all the planes around your current location... and most of all, on all the planes that might interest you.

Michael especially uses these apps a lot:

"Whenever there is a relative or friend coming to visit me, I enter their flight number and I know exactly where they are. This way, I don't have to wait around for them at the airport - I can leave home just in time to pick them up.

The same scenario applies to my own flights - I know if my flight is late, why it's late and how much time I really have. I still can't believe I have access to all this information that was previously limited to air traffic control towers... and now I can see it all on my iPad. Amazing. And very useful."

Maps - Apple vs Google

When Google Maps left the iPad in iOS6 update we were both disappointed. The new Apple maps are not as good as Google Maps were (especially in Europe; they're lacking lots of information) and they're missing our favorite feature of Google Maps - street view. At the time of this writing Google Maps is still only an iPhone app and not a universal app. Google has already announced on Google I/O that the new iPad app is coming this summer and it looks very promising. We can't wait.

Michael also uses Navigon:

"Let's just say that Apple Maps are usually 'good enough'. But for traveling in Europe I also use the Navigon navigation app. Although I prefer to use navigation in my iPhone, it's a very useful app on the iPad to see the route overview and browse the maps quickly. With Navigon, all maps are offline on the iPad."

Booking.com and Expedia

Booking hotels has never been easier. Again, all of the big players like Booking.com or Expedia have great web sites, but their iPad apps are even better!

There's no point in visiting their sites anymore. Just open up one of these apps and find your best hotel for the night. There are additional apps like 'Booking.com tonight' or 'Hotel tonight'.

As this market becomes more competitive, additional players will continue to create fantastic iPad apps. Hotel booking will become easier and easier. For now, between Booking.com and Expedia our hotel needs are set.

The Weather Channel

The iPad doesn't come with a default weather app but there is the Weather Channel app. For obvious reasons you will want to know the weather forecast in the places you travel to and this app is not only very accurate but also very beautiful. Indispensable app for a frequent traveler.

We think this arena is just getting started.

The iPad doesn't come with a default weather app but we prefer the Weather Channel app. For obvious reasons you will want to know the weather forecast for the places you travel to. This app is not only very accurate but also very beautiful.

www.youtube.com/iPadOnlyBook

Video #22: Travelkit - our iPad gear we carry with us when traveling.

Task Management

Every day we need to get stuff done. There are gazillions of task managers out there and on the iOS platform this category is already very crowded. This is how we get our stuff done:

Michael is "eating his own dog-food":

"I'm the founder of Nozbe and it'd be really crazy not to use my own app when working on the iPad. I launched Nozbe more than 6 years ago and I've been using it ever since. When I switched to the iPad we didn't have our own native iPad client, just a third party app and our web app.

Although it wasn't the main reason, one of the motivations for me to work only on the iPad was to accelerate our Nozbe iPad (and mobile) app development and to ensure my team was working in the right direction. Fast forward 12 months and our iPad app is endorsed not only by me, but also by some of the most respected and productive people on the Internet, like Michael Hyatt (famous blogger, the best-selling author of the book 'Platform. Get Noticed in a Noisy World') and others.

Nozbe is an app that loosely follows the GTD (Getting Things Done) methodology coined by the productivity guru David Allen. It's all about managing projects, finding your next actions in these projects, working in contexts and putting everything you need to do into your inbox.

There are a few things that stand out for me when working with Nozbe on my iPad.

First off - collaboration.

With Nozbe we want our customers to learn to 'communicate through tasks'. Stop sending emails back and forth. Create projects, invite people there and add tasks to delegate work between each other. This is what I do - I work in my projects, respond to comments on tasks added by my team and communicate through Nozbe with my peers. We no longer send emails to one another. If we need something done, we just add a task in Nozbe, add a comment to it, delegate it to someone and it's automatically pushed to them.

We believe in the 'less conversation, more action' approach. Thanks to the fact that we have the Nozbe web app, the iPhone and iPad apps and also native apps for most of the platforms out there (Android phones and tablets, Macs and Windows machines) - everyone can join the action. Even if they're not working #iPadOnly like me.

Nozbe has a great 'comments' view where each time someone comments on one of the tasks within the projects I'm sharing with them, I can instantly see the comment and respond when necessary.

Second thing - The Inbox

As with Evernote, Nozbe gives you a unique email address where you can forward emails. In this way, the subject of the email message becomes the task and the contents of the email message become the comment to the task. This also allows me to keep my email inbox and my 'task' inbox separate. When I see an email that is actually a task, I simply forward it to Nozbe and archive it.

Third thing - Nozbe for iPad is as good as the desktop version

Although we're making Nozbe for iPad very touch-friendly and we have to work a lot in order to fit our full desktop

Nozbe to the iPad's screen in the most elegant way possible, we're still getting it done. The iPad version is the fully-featured desktop version of Nozbe, tailored for the iPad. This was important for me - I wanted to have full Nozbe power on my best small computer ever.

As I work #iPadOnly and our entire team has different mobile devices, we keep making Nozbe better. It's our hub for communication and collaboration and getting things done. We're releasing a new Nozbe version each month on all the platforms."

Augusto is the OmniFocus user:

"I have invested hours learning how to do magic with Omnifocus and so much time and energy into making it my platform of choice that it is not really funny anymore (maybe not even productive). It's a really great and powerful app. Do I think it is perfect? The answer it is no.

Actually, I believe that Omnifocus only works when you live on a Mac and iOS devices. If you interact with other platforms, make the jump and use Nozbe; you will find that you will be much more productive.

Omnifocus had a really steep learning curve; it took me years to do what I can do on Omnifocus. Let's be clear, I did the same thing when my platform was on Outlook, I had macros and many more things that would allow me to do things other people didn't think were possible, so it is not that I geek out exclusively in Omnifocus. Whenever I move to a new platform, it is always the same process. What I think is really important is to get to know the tool you use daily very well. Too often, people don't dedicate the time to learn their app and being proficient with it would make them ten times more productive."

We collaborated through Nozbe for this book project.

As we knew there would be many tasks related to our project, we decided to use Michael's platform and created several #iPadOnly related projects in Nozbe. We both enjoyed 'communicating through tasks' there and commenting on our progress.

www.youtube.com/iPadOnlyBook

Video #23: Nozbe on the iPad - how we collaborated on the book.

Augusto's perspective on collaboration in Nozbe:

"I never used Nozbe as my main platform. I tested it when Michael created it and I applaud Michael's success with it. I have always recommended Nozbe to people that want to access their task from any platform because I know how passionate Michael is on the subject of platforms and productivity.

When we decided to write this book, we agreed to maintain the book project in Nozbe. I had no problems doing that because Omnifocus had no way to collaborate with others and I was aware that Nozbe did. I was in for a surprise and a treat.

I love Omnifocus, but for the first time, I have been considering to move just because of this feature. I have been using this book as an excuse to give Michael feedback on those things that I really like about Nozbe and those things that are a must for me.

As much as I may like Omnifocus, the collaboration approach in Nozbe works extremely well. It was not only Michael, we worked with other people on Michael's team and it was all easy to do through Nozbe.

This was something I didn't anticipate when we joined forces for this book. But it is exactly the collaboration part of Nozbe that has me thinking of the possibilities of having my own team in the future to use Nozbe as our 'getting things done' platform. Even as a solo writer you're never actually solo. You have editors, agents, designers and other people working with you. You collaborate. And this is where Nozbe shines."

Mind Mapping

Mind Mapping is a non-linear way of brainstorming that allows you to attach related items to each other even if they're not in a logical sequence. It's a very visual tool for planning and seeing your goals. We both use mind mapping a lot.

Michael started mind-mapping in college:

"I love mind-mapping. It started in college when I had to write my Master Thesis - I didn't know to approach it, an outline felt too 'limiting'. Then I heard about mind-mapping. So I started drawing my first mind maps. Finally, when I got the hang of it, I drew a large mind-map of my entire thesis on my dorm-room wall. While drawing mind-maps on paper is fun, it's even more fun on the iPad."

Michael uses iThoughtsHD:

"This is the app I use for my mind-mapping needs. I use Mind Maps to brainstorm ideas and most importantly to write down my goals for the weeks and months to come.

I prefer to have my projects and tasks in my task-manager of choice (Nozbe) - this is where the real, actionable stuff is. The more abstract stuff like goal planning and new project brainstorming happens in the mind-maps.

I love iThoughtsHD because it's a very mature and versatile application and syncs with Dropbox. The files that it saves in Dropbox are compatible with many desktop clients (like Xmind, Freemind and other apps) so I can easily access my mind-maps on my Mac if I need to."

Augusto uses MindJet Mind Manager:

"I have been mind-mapping for at least ten years. I discovered mind-mapping as a useful tool when I was doing my MBA in 2001. One of my friends was a fanatic mind-mapper so as a geek I spent hours looking for software to handle the task. The truth is I can't read my own handwriting!

I discovered Mindjet MindManager and participated in the beta testing of MindManager 7 and 8 for Mac and PC. I have been a customer ever since. When they released the version for the iPad, I jumped onboard and have never looked back.

I like MindManager to visualize hard concepts and solve complex problems. Once I have found the invisible connections I then move to a regular outline to work."

Visual Maps and Vision Goals with Mind Mapping software

The other thing we use Mind Mapping software for is to work with 'visual maps' or create 'vision boards'.

www.youtube.com/iPadOnlyBook

Video #24: Mind Mapping and Vision Boards on the iPad.

Augusto loves creating his Vision Boards:

I don't remember when I made my first visual map, but I have made many over the years. I love to create images of the things I dream of accomplishing and to do that I create vision boards. I am not a very artistic person so I really enjoy the fact that I don't need to use scissors or glue - just copy and paste. Also, since they are for private consumption, I can google and find images on the web and pull in any that I think will be appropriate.

In some instances where I want to think and use a bigger screen, I use the iPad in conjunction with the Apple TV and the mirroring function. It is absolutely amazing to have the iPad in your lap and work with it on the big screen while you are mind-mapping."

Grafio

Sometimes what we need is not a mind-map but something even less linear, like a flow chart. For instance, when we needed to design new workflows for the iPad, we wanted an app for just that. Grafio is amazing. It's very natural, very easy to use and very touch-friendly; perfect for the iPad. We draw all of the workflows there and later export them to Evernote via email.

When Michael discovered this app, he never looked back:

essence of working on the iPad. Drawing diagrams with it feels natural - like drawing on paper... but the app corrects you and makes sure your shapes and arrows are beautiful and flexible.

Yes, flexible. You can edit and move objects and arrows attached to them anywhere you want, draw new ones, and so on. Before I discovered Grafio I used to draw my diagrams in a drawing app on the iPad like Paper... but it was just like drawing on a piece of paper - once something is drawn, it was hard to edit it and move around. You'd have to erase it and draw again. With Grafio, I get the beauty of drawing and the natural feeling that comes with it along with the flexibility of a vector drawing app and the versatility of the iPad."

Augusto fell in love with Grafio as well:

"Grafio is one of the really cool things I learned while writing this book. When Michael shared this application with me, I immediately started drawing diagrams and creating workflows. The application helps you think and visualize problems in an easy, quick and intuitive way.

I am not in any way an expert on this application, but it is an app that I am enjoying and learning more and more about every day."

Touch and solve your problems!

OK, it sounds a little corny, but we have discovered that using apps for mind-mapping and workflow design on the iPad really helps solve bigger problems and brainstorm new ideas. The feeling of moving things around with fingers, zooming, swiping and tapping makes everything 'more real' and the apps we mentioned in this chapter make the whole process fun and natural.

www.youtube.com/iPadOnlyBook

Video #25: Diagrams and Brainstorming with Grafio on the iPad.

Learning

Without a doubt, the iPad excels as a learning machine. There are so many educative titles for everyone to enjoy and learn from. And it doesn't apply just to the adults. We're both fathers and we want our children to learn as much as possible as well. It's even better if they can learn while they are playing.

Augusto loves to teach her daughter with an iPad:

"The number of educational apps for the iPad is incredible. My daughter is reading books and playing with apps that teach her how to write, read and think. I even noticed some apps are growing with her as she develops more skills and knowledge.

Adults are served well, too. Apart from the iTunes University, which has an incredible amount of knowledge available, there are apps to help you acquire any skill. I mentioned many times in this book that you can learn how to touch-type on the iPad's screen with the TapTyping app. Now that I got my iPad mini, I'm using this app again to improve my speed on the smaller screen. The progress I'm making is amazing. All thanks to this app."

Michael also lets his children play and learn on the iPad:

"My children use the iPad to learn to write, read, do puzzles, build robots and do other amazing stuff. I encourage you to find out more about the apps that can help your children learn something today.

As for me, apps like TapTyping or Reading Trainer help me improve the skills I know I need to improve."

Here's just a short list of the applications both we and our kids use for learning on the iPad. There are many more. Be sure to do some research and find the ones that suit you best:

* TapTyping
* Reading Trainer
* iBooks
* Kindle
* TED
* Bob Books
* First Words (English and Spanish)
* Montessori Alphabet
* Montessori Words
* Math Garden
* Intro to letters
* Khan Academy
* Where's My Water
* iReading Books
* ABC Magnetic Toys
* JumpStart my ABC
* Sandra Boynton's Books/apps
* Doctor Seuss' Books/Apps
* TocaBoca games

A few noteworthy apps we use very often

We'll finish this chapter by diving a little deeper into the apps we particularly like and use a lot.

TapTyping

We use this app to learn to touch-type on both the external keyboard as well as the on-screen keyboard of the iPad.

Michael was totally blown away by this app:

"While I already knew how to touch-type before my switch to the iPad, I managed to improve my writing speeds by training on the external keyboard.

But what really struck me was that I could actually learn how to touch type on the on-screen keyboard of the iPad! When Augusto recommended this app to me I couldn't believe it, but the results I got were amazing.

When I started, I could type 20 WPM (words per minute) on the on-screen keyboard vs 60 WPM on the external keyboard. Now I can type up to 70 WPM on the external keyboard vs 50 WPM on the on-screen keyboard! Almost as fast! All thanks to this app."

Augusto is convinced everyone should take their time to learn how to type:

"I think the ability to type fast is one of the most useful tricks that one can do to improve their productivity. I dedicated an entire chapter to this in my book '25 Tips for Productivity'. Just think about it, you can easily double or even triple your writing speeds, saving you hours each day.

TapTyping was the solution I took to learn to type on the screen of the iPad. I was really slow, to the point that I even considered getting rid of the iPad if I could not solve that problem. I started practicing and learned some really cool tricks in the process.

I am not as fast on the screen as I am with a keyboard, but I can type more than 60 words per minute on the screen of the iPad."

www.youtube.com/iPadOnlyBook

Video #26: Touch-typing on the iPad thanks to TapTyping app.

ReadQuick

The idea behind Read Quick is that it shows you only one word on the screen at a time.

Augusto likes this app a lot:

"This interesting concept worked much better on my iPad Mini than the regular iPad for one simple reason: weight. As with many of the things I tried, just reading one word on the screen helped me tremendously in regards to staying focused. ReadQuick connects with Instapaper inbox where I can read my 'saved for later' articles through the app. It also measures the speed of my reading and gives me an estimate of how much time it will take me to read an article. This serves me really well as I am constantly under-estimating my reading time."

TED

We both love TED talks and have been listening to them for years. It's great that they have a fantastic app for the iPad. Over the last few years TED grew and they licensed people to do TEDx in many cities all over the world (TEDx is an independent TED event). We both were invited to speak at TEDx events -Michael in 2010 at TEDx Warsaw and Augusto in 2013 at TEDx Fort Wayne.

TED talks have a special place on our iPads, we watch them mostly for inspiration. The application allows us to save favorite talks, share them, save them for watching offline and even to retrieve a random talk.

With TED talks you learn and are inspired to aim a little higher. To get out of your comfort zone. To reach for more. With this app, our iPad becomes our 'inspiration device'.

You learn, you grow... with the iPad.

There are so many titles for learning on the iPad that it'd be impossible for us to review them all here. That's why we encourage you to dig deeper and find the apps that will help you and your kids grow, learn and get inspired.

There is a scene in the movie 'Matrix' when Neo asks Trinity if she knows how to fly a helicopter and she says she doesn't... yet. And then they upload a program directly to her brain and she instantly has the skills to fly the machine. This is how we feel about the iPad. Do you want to learn something? Well, 'there is an app for that'.

Parenting

Being a parent is the most fulfilling and gratifying job on earth. Having children is like discovering completely new feelings you never thought you had.

In the last chapter we discussed how the iPad can be used for learning - for both adults and children. In this chapter, let's take this thought a little deeper and talk how the iPad really helps with parenting.

Augusto's children learn on iPad:

"In my household we try to push for educational applications over games. Our daughter knows how to play with the iPad but we like her to use it to learn rather than play. Because of that we decided to give her a LeapFrog LeapPad device for games. I have always been a believer that you should separate your working and playing tools, and it is for that reason that we decided to teach her to see the LeapPad as a game tool and use the iPad mostly for learning. Our iPads have learning apps as well as books that are appropriate for her age. On the other hand, it is a constant challenge because she would prefer to play on the iPad. The good thing is, because she knows that her father works on the iPad, she is able to see the iPad more as a 'work' rather than 'play' device."

Michael dedicated one old iPad 1 as a play and learn device:

"My 4-year old loves the iPad. She plays games, does puzzles, plays memory games, keeps drawings, sketches and the like... and watches Pixar movies (she's currently into 'Wall-e' and wants to be called Eva).

If you're a parent it's great to investigate the apps available for kids. Especially the apps related to the movies and shows they are watching every day. Most of them are not games alone but carefully constructed educational apps that are themed with things like 'Hello Kitty', 'Cars', 'Thomas and Friends', and the like.

I watch my girl and see which movies she really likes and later get her the educational apps that match the theme. For example, we have a few 'Thomas and Friends' apps on the iPad and they include puzzles, memory games, short movies, drawing exercises... and so much more.

I had an old iPad 1st generation and I configured it entirely for my daughter. I advise many parents to go to eBay and get an old iPad 1 and configure it for their kids. It's an inexpensive toy and so much fun. And get the Apple's cover for the iPad. The black cover. Otherwise, the kids will totally kill the machine by dropping it accidentally."

Warning - iPad-free days for kids

The problem with the iPad is that it can be addictive for kids. It is a great trick to calm down a 4-year old by giving her an iPad but you have to watch out. We've found out that we needed to put strict rules in place like: 'you will only play for one hour today' or 'today we don't play with the iPad'. If we fail to put these rules in place, the child loses interest in anything else and only looks for the iPad and asks for it all of the time.

"Parental controls" to the rescue

Plus, it's good to put the 'Parental controls' in place and disable in-app-purchases for the kids as well as new apps purchases (all available in iPad's settings). Many games for kids have hidden options to buy more... you don't want your kid to burn your credit card now do you?

In the same way that we need to use self-control toward our devices, we need to teach our kids to exercise control when using our devices (or their devices).If we don't teach them to use their devices to work and learn how can we expect them to discover a better way?

www.youtube.com/iPadOnlyBook

Video #27: Using iPad with kids - parental advice from two fathers.

Apps for both kids and parents

Just like our parents used to play table games with us, we can use the iPad to play with our kids It can be used to read interactive books to them, and to show them the world through the magical, 'touchy' screen of the iPad.

As we mentioned in the last chapter about learning, parents can find fantastic apps on the iPad to help them learn, grow, play and watch movies.

We have the first eighteen years of our kids lives to provide them with the tools that help them grow and get the most out of the experiences in life and more importantly so that after the moment they reach eighteen they can continue growing and being productive.

Entertainment

The iPad comes integrated with the Apple's iTunes Store and it is the go-to place to buy digital content on the iPad.

Movies

Michael tries not to buy movies anymore:

'My wife still buys movies. She's very sentimental and likes to keep some of the classics. That's why I got her the 64GB iPad Mini - so that she could buy and preload the iPad with the movies she buys.

I rent movies. This is especially handy when traveling. When I'm at home, I rent movies directly through the Apple TV and stream them there. However, when I need to travel, I rent the movies directly on my iPad and download them there. This way, for longer trips I have a few movies on my iPad ready to be watched during the evening in a hotel room. I don't have to depend on the hotel's movie offerings or flaky Internet connection.

Here's what happens - when you rent a movie on the iPad, it's downloaded entirely to your device. You have it, it's ready to be watched. Now, the cool thing is, you have 30 days to watch it. When you're traveling and you want to watch the movie, you open up iTunes and connect to the Internet to authorize the movie to be played on your iPad. Once authorized, the movie plays offline directly from your device. It's really cool, even if you're on a cellular connection, you can authorize the movie to play and you don't have to worry about your data quota. You can go offline and still watch the movie. You have 24 hours to watch once the movie has been authorized."

Augusto on Movies:

"We used to have a large movie collection, but now we rent from Apple if the movie is not available on Amazon or Netflix.

Even though the iPad has a great screen to watch movies and videos, I personally don't have much use for this feature. I tend to consume much more of the written word that anything else, so I don't spend really much time watching videos. I have seen a movie or two but it isn't something I really do with any regularity.

Instead, when I sit in front of a TV, I can say that my iPad is the best remote ever for DirectTV, Netflix and Hulu. Nothing beats the iPad applications together with an Apple TV in the ability to interact with these platforms."

TV Shows

Michael watches TV shows only on Hulu and

Netflix:

"Apple really killed that one for my wife and I. We used to rent TV shows for $0.99 on iTunes and it was great. One buck per episode was the best price ever. Now you can only buy TV shows. Three bucks each. Too expensive. Why would we want to buy a TV show? I'd watch it once and that's it. We very rarely, if ever, would go back to an episode of even our favorite shows. We might understand a reason to buy a movie, but a TV show? Nope, not buying. You'll find us streaming through Netflix or Hulu."

Netflix, Hulu and Amazon

We are both subscribers of Hulu Plus, Amazon and Netflix and this is how we watch movies and TV shows. It's actually funny we'd call them 'TV shows' as we never watch them on a cable TV. Yes, when you're at home I'm watching these on a TV screen through the Apple TV device... but when not at home their respective iPad apps come to the rescue.

We love how Netflix works. They've nailed the streaming mechanisms so well that even with traveling and poor Internet speeds, you can still watch Netflix very comfortably. And because Netflix has a fantastic library of TV shows, there is always something interesting to watch.

Michael is a big fan of Netflix but hates their app's "content discovery" options:

"The only problem with the Netflix app is that they mix TV shows with movies. I mean, if I want to watch a movie (i.e. I have ~ 2 hours of free time) I want to easily see the upcoming movies, the top movies now, the new releases, etc... and for some reason they mix both of them together and I find it hard to search for movies to watch. It's better done on iTunes.

We also like Hulu Plus. Especially the current episodes of the TV shows - they appear on Hulu the next day, the same as they appeared on the cable TV. The only downside are the number of, ahem, stupid ads. I don't mind the fact that the ads are there so much - I understand it's Hulu's business model... I'd just welcome less stupid ads... but maybe I'm just picky."

Augusto is also a big fan of Amazon:

"Amazon - the last player in this section is also offering TV shows and movies for rent (or free if you are an Amazon Prime member) - it's not yet at par with Netflx and HuluPlus but it is catching up quickly."

Movie Trailers and IMDB

Michael loves watching movie trailers and he's doing it mainly on the iPad:

"I love the Apple's Movie Trailers app as well as the IMDB - Internet Movie Database - both apps are amazing for discovering new movies, getting to know the cast, the stories and user comments. Whenever I want to rent a movie on iTunes or watch something on Netflix, I fire up the IMDB app to check its ratings and see if it's worth my time."

Yes, iPad is a fantastic entertainment device.

It's lightweight; you can hold it on a sofa or couch, watch whatever you want, stream to your TV through your Apple TV and so much more. We'd say you can safely go #iPadOnly as far as entertainment is concerned.

Gaming

This is the part where you'll have to find better experts than us. We really don't have the time to play games and we aren't very passionate gamers anyway. We'd rather read a book or watch a movie when we have some free time. Michael's wife plays solitaire on her iPad: 'but she's a solitaire-maniac - she can't be helped.'

Suffice to say, there are more games than any other apps in the App Store. So again, you can go #iPadOnly as far as gaming is concerned. Paired with Apple TV streaming, things get even better.

Michael sometimes plays games:

"Yes, I sometimes play (although not all that much). I do some racing like the F1 Racing and Grand Theft Auto. I play F1 racing before each Forumula 1 Grand Prix to see how the track 'feels' and to get to know the track from the driver's perspective. The GTA games bring back memories from when I was in college and I used to spend hours playing this game on the PC. Oh yes, and I sometimes play NBA live as well - but I have this one on my iPhone and use it to 'kill time' when I'm waiting somewhere for someone."

Augusto doesn't install games at all:

"Because I know how easy I can get distracted, my iPad does not contain any games. The iPad is my main working machine, if I add games to it, I will no longer be productive on my iPad.

Recently in the US, Starbucks gave away the Angry Birds Star Wars edition and since I'm a big Star Wars fan I installed it on my iPhone and wasted quite a few hours."

If you're into Gaming - iPad is your thing

With the iPad's big screen and the retina graphics of the big iPad, it's a fantastic and very engaging gaming device. Add Game Center to it and you'll be playing with everyone you know in no time.

Again, we use the iPads as our work machines so we try to avoid the games. We have our kids to play with and we have our wives to watch movies with. However, you can play if you want - be our guest.

Handy Apps

There are many apps that are really handy on the iPad and or the iPhone but that may not be enough to have their own category per se, so we decided to group them here and write at least a short paragraph about how we use them.

Apple Notes

Augusto still uses this built-in app:

"When Apple released their Notes application on the first iPhone, I was really mad (and complained a lot) that it did not include categories, or tags or anything else to manage my Notes. Over the years I have made peace with this. The cool part is the fact that it is connected to iCloud, so any change can be accessed by my iPad, iPhone and Mac. And recently, the ability to search Notes has improved significantly. You can use iPad's global search to find a Note you're looking for."

Michael doesn't use Apple Notes all that much:

"I do all of my note taking on Evernote.

Contacts and Calendar

We both use the built-in Contacts and Calendar apps and we love the way they sync with the iCloud and with our family members. In one of the later chapters in this book Michael will explain how he syncs his iCloud with his wife's and shares the calendars together.

This is what Augusto thinks about these apps:

"I have trusted my Calendar since 1995. That was the year I got my first PalmPilot. Over the years my calendar has evolved and improved. Today, my personal, work and family Calendars live in iCloud. I love using colors for each calendar. Each work calendar, personal calendar as well as every member of our family gets its own color. It helps identify each activity even without reading the detailed info.

What I love about the Calendar on the iPad more than anything else is the week view. In general I don't use any other view on the calendar on the iPad. I am aware that you can do the same on the iPhone, but even with the bigger screen of the iPhone, it is not as comfortable to work and plan as it is on the iPad.

As with the calendars, my contacts are also in iCloud. I love to have them sync to every device without any effort on my part. In the years of the Palm, I had categories for those contacts but now I just leave keywords in the note field of the contact so I can find the information quickly by simply using the search function."

Apple Airport Utility

Augusto is very grateful for this little app:

"All of my Wi-Fi routers are Apple Airports that together work to extend the network so we can access them all around the house. Before Apple released this little application, it was simply impossible to manage my Apple Airports on the iPad or the iPhone - you always needed a Mac or a PC.

This application allows me to update, restart and configure my Apple Airport Wi-Fi network in a really easy way. It's not an application I use daily but I am really grateful that I no longer need a Mac to configure my Airport network."

Banking Apps

We have mixed experiences with our Online Banking Applications

We both try not to physically visit our banks. Instead, we use online banking to manage our finances. With the iPad it's getting even easier.

Augusto's take on the banking apps in iPad:

"I live in the USA. There are many banks with applications on the iPad. In my case I use Bank of America and WellsFargo.

I really like the fact that I can use their applications, which allow me to pay bills, transfer money, deposit checks and more, all in the comfort of the sofa and the ease of the iPad. I can't put my finger on why the apps work better than their respective web sites, but in my experience, they do.

Michael still prefers his bank's web sites:

"My case is different. My banks are in Europe - Barclays in Spain, mBank and other banks in Poland. All of them have iPad apps at the time of this writing, but these are still very basic. They also make the authentication really painful as they ask me to remember both my usernames and passwords to log in for security reasons. That's why I prefer to use 1Password and log into their web sites on the iPad and manage everything from there. However, I'm sure the future of 'appification' will also reach my Internet banks and their apps will improve as well."

Soulver

Michael found a new type of calculator in this app:

"When I initially wrote this chapter I complained about the lack of the built-in calculator app on the iPad and the fact that I needed one and that I found one in an app called 'Calculator Pro'. Well, it's all irrelevant now.

The thing is, the built-in calculator app on the iPhone, as well as the Calculator Pro app on the iPad try to replicate the old calculator machines... without taking into account that we live in the 21st century and have a much more versatile and capable machine now - the iPad.

To my surprise, there is an app that takes advantage of the iPad and works in a totally different league than the old-school calculator - the app is called Soulver. It's a notepad with a built-in calculator that can be used somewhat as a spreadsheet. I know, it sounds complicated but it isn't - you just have to get this app to see what I mean. Suffice to say, all of my calculating needs, as well as currency conversions, are done by this app. Just get it - this is what a calculator for an iPad (and iPhone) should look and work like."

Apple Cards

Augusto convinced Michael to give this app a try:

"This is another Apple application that I use constantly. I love the idea that I can take a picture (or use one of my pictures) and send a card to anyone. Like a postcard with my kids' photo to their grandparents. This makes the process both convenient and inexpensive. Michael didn't know about this app but now he's sold on the concept as well."

Video #28: Apple Cards - send cards directly from your iPad.

Clipboard Manager and History

This app makes copying and pasting a little more convenient according to Michael:

"One of the few things I was really missing from my 'computer life' before going #iPadOnly was a way of copying many things to the clipboard at once... (which I did on my Mac using a third-party app) and pasting them later..

When the iPhone initially launched, it didn't have a Clipboard at all... now the iOS has Clipboard but I wish it was more versatile. Once you copy something there... and then you copy something else, the first thing disappears forever.

Thanks to the Clipboard History app I can almost replicate my PC flow here. I open up the app and for a few minutes, the app is monitoring everything I copy to Clipboard and is saving it in the app. I can select a piece of text, copy it, select another one, copy it again, and copy something else... and I know all of this is being saved in the app.

Later when I want to paste this information, I just go to the app, click on something and it's copied to clipboard again and I can paste it wherever I want.

This is still not ideal. I'd rather have a more robust Clipboard with full history integrated directly to the iOS (and ideally synced with other devices through iCloud) but it's sufficient for now.

The thing is, after so many years of OSX and iOS one would think they'd enhance the Clipboard to boost our productivity... but they didn't. Thankfully we have apps for that."

www.youtube.com/iPadOnlyBook

Video #29: The clipboard history app - how to handle multiple copy and paste on the iPad.

Explain Everything

This app allows you to use videos, pictures and your current screen of the iPad and create interactive explanations of what you're doing. Michael is using this app to explain things to his team and Augusto uses it to explain things to his family. We're also recording some videos with this app to post on our #iPadOnly web site.

Find my Phone

Find My Phone it is something that any user of iPhone, iPad or iPodTouch should activate. Not only is it great to find your device around your house, (the most common use in our households) it is a powerhouse should your device go missing. Find My Phone allows you to see where the device is, change the password and more.

It is really a great tool, especially because we all have delicate and confidential information on our devices. This app allows you to remotely delete or lock your device. That's why we strongly recommend, if you have an iOS device (and we assume you have as you're reading this book), please get this app and activate this service. Better safe than sorry.

LogMeIn

This is an app that turns the iPad into a real Mac remote control. Michael uses it a lot:

"When I'm far away from home but need to perform something on my Mac... or when I'm in my bedroom and still need to do an administrative task on my Mac... I use LogMeIn Ignition app to do it directly from the iPad. This app lets me tap on my Mac's screen through the iPad's screen.

OK, I must admit that now I'm more than a year working almost exclusively on my iPad so my use of this app has decreased substantially in the last 12 months. I find it harder and harder to have a task I need to perform on my Mac that I can't do on my iPad. However, if such a thing shows up, it's convenient to quickly access my Mac's desktop via LogMeIn and see my desktop screen and do what needs to get done."

Augusto also uses LogMeIn:

"I have been using LogMeIn for a long, long time. Having my parents living in another country and being their tech support person made me turn to this app. Before the iPad I also used it to access my personal computer from work. When I got my iPad and LogMeIn released their Ignition application it was a no brainer for me. It is honestly an application that I don't use often, but that every time I do, I can't express how happy I am to have it. My MacBook is on all the time since it is the iTunes hub in our house. I can manage it remotely with my iPad and LogMeIn.

In my opinion, LogMeIn on the iPad is not robust enough to use your iPad as a terminal to work on your remote computer in a permanent way. It is not necessarily LogMeIn's fault and more the need to use the mouse for many things on the Computer. I am sure there are people that would make that work, as I am sure that if I needed to do it for a short period of time I would do it, but in general it is not a substitute for the computer.

That said, it is great for when you need to access your Mac for something quick, find documents, and do simple and quick things on the MacBook when I am out and about.

While I was writing this, I was trying to remember when was the last time that I accessed my MacBook using LogMeIn Ignition and I could not remember. The reality is that I have migrated most of my file structure to the cloud, and because of that I have needed this app less and less. Most likely the reason to keep it on the iPad is to do support for my parents' computers. Anyway, I still believe it's great to have this app just in case."

OmniOutliner

Michael doesn't use this app but Augusto swears by it:

"I do visual maps, mind-maps and outlines constantly. Every book that I have written (including this one) began in an outline. I have never found a more complete solution than

OmniOutliner. I can use multiple files, and add/remove information as needed in the outline until it is ready for prime time or until I am ready to begin writing. At that time, I move the outline in text form to Scrivener in the Mac where I create the folder structure that will sync to the iPad, ready for me to write.

If you need or like to use outlines, this application is probably the most powerful tool you are going to find to accomplish that."

Paprika

Augusto recommends this app for cooking:

"My wife loves to cook. A couple of years ago I got her this app - it is a recipe application and nothing more. It shows you how to add ingredients and prepare the meal with beautiful pictures. It even allows you to adjust the amount of a recipe automatically. Let's say you want to cook something for one person instead of two. Paprika will adjust your ingredients and will calculate the correct amounts.

You can automatically extract many recipes from the web, make meal plans, categorize the recipes you have created and build your list for groceries.

My wife used to own many recipe books, but instead of looking through those for hours, she is now using Paprika to prepare our meals."

Prompt

This is a very geeky app, but important if you're running your own server, or a server infrastructure like Michael does at Nozbe:

"As a CEO of an Internet company I'm wearing many hats. Over time, I finally got many great and talented people to replace me in programming, system administration and other tactical duties. But as mentioned in my chapter about Textastic, every now and then I step back into one of these roles. I sometimes code and I sometimes need to log in to one of our servers just to see if everything's all right without asking my CTO about it. He's got too much on his plate anyway.

To access our Linux-based servers via SSH I use an app called Prompt. People who have been using the 'Terminal' app on the Mac will feel at home with this one. People who don't know what the Terminal app is for on the Mac, will have no idea what I'm talking about.

To be fair to the latter group, and probably the majority of the readers of this book, I'll stop right there. If you need a Terminal replacement on your iPad, just get Prompt.'

QuoteBook

Augusto likes to get inspired with this app:

"I love Quotes. I always have. I always will. QuoteBook is one of those cool applications that allow you to sort, search and 'manage' quotes from the people you find inspiring.

Using this app allows me not only to get inspired but also to explain things in the words of other people.

I use this application extensively, not only to share inspiring quotes on Twitter but I also store those tweets that I want to share more than once. For example, I store snippets from my books or information on the sales of my books."

Drop Manager

As mentioned numerous times in this book, we're both fans of Dropbox as one of our 'cloud solutions' for going #iPadOnly. However, the native Dropbox app, as much as it has improved over the years, still requires you to go to their web site to perform basic administrative functions. Michael doesn't like it:

"I hate it that to rename, move or in any other way manage my files in Dropbox I need to go their web site which is not touch-friendly at all. Thankfully there is an app for that, too. I use Drop Manager for Dropbox - an app that fills in all these blanks. I can rename files and folders easily, copy them, move them around, you name it.

OK, the app is not very pretty and its design leaves something to be desired so there is a little bit of a learning curve to using it, but once you get the hang of it, it's very useful. That's it in a nutshell. This app is just useful and I use it almost daily."

Scanner Pro

How Augusto's iPad turned into a scanner:

"I used to travel with NeatReceipt tucked in my bag. It wasn't big, but required the Mac in order to work. Since I no longer carry the Mac and I am mostly on the iPad, I began looking for a solution to solve that problem. My solution is an application called Scanner Pro. The app not only takes a picture of the document, but also performs a bit of image-rendering magic to ensure it's as legible as can be. I think it is really incredible that I can scan a document anywhere, convert to PDF and send it without anyone knowing that I simply did all that on my iPad."

TextExpander

Take your keyboard snippets to the next level - here's why Michael uses this app all of the time:

"In the chapter about iPad's keyboard (or the lack of it) I talked about the built-in keyboard shortcuts in the iOS. These are great but they are all one-liners. Meaning, if you'd like to define a keyboard shortcut for your entire physical address, or for an email signature or for anything else that requires more than one line, you'd have to define multiple keyboard shortcuts.

In TextExpander, things are different. You can define as a single keyboard shortcut an entire email message, a template of a document or anything else for that matter. I use it often to create templates. For example, a template for a blog post, for an email message, for a paragraph, a chapter, a list of links, and much, much more.

The only problem is that TextExpander is a third party app so only some of the iOS apps (and none of the Apple's apps) support it. However, most writing apps do (like Byword, Nebulous Notes, AI Writer…). That's why for my writing purposes, I have created many TextExpander snippets and use them almost every day.

My best advice is for you is start with creating a blog post template if you're a blogger. I just type 'msblog' and my entire blog post is filled in with all the parts of the blog post I need to include. Extremely useful."

YouTube

You Tube it is the standard of video. You may like it or not. You may like or dislike Google, but the reality is that You Tube is one of the most important search engines, and you may be surprised on how many answers you can find there.

Yes, you can do YouTube on the browser, or you can use their application. It really depends on how many videos you view on YouTube and how much you like the extra features that the app offers, such as the favorites or the watch later features.

Augusto likes the YouTube app but Michael prefers to watch the YouTube videos in the browser as he manages his YouTube channels there and wants to make sure he has all the functionality in place to do so.

There's an app for what you need, too!

In this chapter we covered the most notable 'Handy Apps' we use and primarily wanted to convince you that there is an app for almost anything on the iPad.

According to Apple there are almost 400,000 apps that are designed specifically for the iPad in the Apple App Store (out of 900,000 apps in total). This makes the iPad a very mature platform that can tackle almost every problem and help you jump on the #iPadOnly bandwagon. The best part, most of these apps are not only useful, but very focused, touch-friendly and just pure fun to use.

CHAPTER #5
WHY IPHONE MATTERS WHEN YOU'RE GOING #IPADONLY

When the iPhone launched in 2007, the author of the "Innovator's Dillema" - Clayton Christensen said the iPhone would fail, because it didn't disrupt the cellular phones, it just made them better. We are sure that Mr Christensen doesn't want to be reminded of that comment. He even corrected himself 5 years later when he said he didn't realize the iPhone did disrupt something totally else - it disrupted portable computers.

This is what the iPhone really is. A portable computer that we have in our pocket at all times... and this computer happens to also be able to make a phone call.

Augusto is totally amazed by his iPhone's capabilities:

"The iPhone brings more power than my first laptop, it is really an incredible world of possibilities in my pocket and it is exactly that which makes it a blessing or a curse depending on how much I can apply self-discipline and work with my own temptations."

The iPhone is great, but Michael knows the iPad is not just a bigger iPhone:

'Think about it for a moment. The iPhone came first. The iPad came later. When the iPad shipped, people were saying it was just a 'bigger iPhone' or 'bigger iPod touch'. It's true to the same extent that an Olympic swimming pool is just a 'bigger Jacuzzi'.

The iPhone has become my perfect companion to my iPad and when I'm working #iPadOnly - it's an indispensable device. Even when the iPad is my main machine, I continue to use my iPhone a lot as well."

Is the iPhone mirror device or a complimentary one?

We believe that the iPhone compliments the iPad. Many apps are universal and are optimized for both platforms. That's why in most cases we install the same apps on the iPhone that we already have on the iPad. This way we can start our work on the iPad and continue on the iPhone when needed. However, you have to be careful with that - iPhone can serve as a real distractor because of (or thanks to) its power and app availability.

Here's Augusto's take on this problem:

'There are many people that use their iPads without an iPhone, but I am much more aware of people with both devices. The reality is that the iPhone complements the iPad really well. So well in fact that it sometimes distracts me instead of pushing me to focus and accomplish more. It all depends how you design your workflows and which kinds of tasks you're trying to get done on each device. As mentioned before, I purposefully decided not to configure email on my iPhone as I noticed I was checking it too frequently without actually processing it.

For me the iPad is my main machine and I have different apps on my iPad's home screen than on my iPhone's. The latter is here to mostly provide me with portable access to my information."

Michael has a 50/30/20 rule:

"To give you an idea of how I work I invented a 50/30/20 rule, meaning I do 50% of my tasks only on the iPad and don't even touch the iPhone for them (like writing and other 'content creation' tasks), 30% on both the iPhone and the iPad (like email and communication via FaceTime, Skype or iMessage) and 20% of the tasks only on the iPhone This includes taking pictures and recording videos, not to mention the old-school phone calls which can only be done on the iPhone. There are exceptions to this rule but this 50/30/20 is my own iPad-iPhone usage pattern.

I also have my iPhone and iPad home screens configured with practically the same apps. You might think this goes a little contrary to the above-mentioned rule but bear with me. It just gives me the convenience that whichever device I take, the same app appears in the same place so I don't have to think where it is. I just tap away."

Can you go #iPadOnly without the iPhone?

Some have tried, but as to most questions, the answer is 'it depends on what you do'.

However, we believe it'd be really hard to do and won't give you the same benefits we mention in this book. The power of having the same ecosystem on your main machine and on your phone is so amazing that to really be able to go #iPadOnly and be very productive you need to have both the iPhone and the iPad.

www.youtube.com/iPadOnlyBook

Video #30: Why the iOS ecosystem is so important for the iPad and the iPhone.

7 Benefits of having an iPhone with your #iPadOnly setup.

As we said the iPad and the iPhone complement each other extremely well and can make you exceptionally productive in your #iPadOnly journey. Here are the 7 benefits of having both in your toolbox:

1) The same look and feel

Both devices are multi-touch devices where you can use them in both horizontal and vertical mode. You use your built-in stylus (i.e. finger) to navigate both of them. It just feels natural.

2) The same operating system

Both the iPad and the iPhone run iOS. There's no learning curve, no problem with syncing, compatibility or anything else. The iPad can run any iPhone app and most of these are already universal and are optimized for both devices. Having two devices that behave the same way and have similar apps really helps.

3) The same (or similar) apps

Speaking of the apps - while there are some iPhone or iPad specific apps on our devices, most of the apps we use every day are designed for both- again - a huge productivity boost.

4) The sync

Thanks to Dropbox, iCloud, Evernote, Nozbe and other 'clouds' we use, everything is perfectly synced between our iPhones and iPads. Through the air, with the cloud. No cables, no nothing. It just works. We can start something on the iPad and finish it on the go with the iPhone. It's that easy. Clean. Fast. Efficient.

5) Internet connection all of the time

Even if your iPad is Wi-Fi only, you can always tether your Internet connection from the iPhone. This way your #iPadOnly machine can be online anytime you want.

Actually, Augusto and Michael approach the Internet connection argument differently. Augusto uses Wi-Fi only on his iPad on purpose - he's a writer so he prefers not to be distracted when he writes. Michael has a Cellular iPad and he loves the fact that his main computer is connected to the Internet all of the time. Anywhere. No more searching for Wi-Fi hotspots, it's always online wherever he goes.

6) The iPhone can substitute the iPad

We don't even have to take our iPads everywhere. Although it's very portable and fits into a man-purse, you can simply rely on the iPhone when you go out... and have more-or-less the same 'office' in your pocket.

Of course, for a longer period of time, it's a lot better to work on the big, gorgeous iPad screen. That's why we're working #iPadOnly and not #iPhoneOnly.

Again, while there are tasks we normally wouldn't do on the iPhone and would do only on the iPad... because both have the same apps and OS, we *CAN* do the same tasks if we really needed to. Thanks to all the points above, the iPad is our office now, and the iPhone is the smaller version of this office which is in our pockets at all times. Sweet.

7) The same chargers and other accessories

Michael upgraded to iPhone 5 and iPad 4 in order to have the same 'Lightning' cable for both devices. Augusto has iPhone 5 and iPad Mini, also with the same cables. Other than that, both the iPhone and the iPad share a few accessories (and we'll talk more on those in the next chapters of the book). It's very practical.

Michael adds a bonus point to our list:

"Now that I'm working #iPadOnly, I find I'm also more productive on the iPhone. I had all of the generations of the iPhone before and I knew a lot about the iOS and how to use it, but thanks to being #iPadOnly now, I squeeze a lot more productivity from the iPhone. Again, because it's configured the same way as my iPad."

It's just great to be #iPadOnly with an iPhone

The iPhone and the iPad work together really well and complement each other tremendously, making the iPhone-iPad combo a greater tool than the sum of its parts.

The iPhone as a second screen

We both love the iPad for its many productivity-oriented features, especially the 'one-app-screen-at-a-time paradigm' which helps you focus on the thing you have to get done at the moment.

For 80% of the tasks it's great, but sometimes you just need a second screen to be able to have some 'reference' material running alongside your work and glance at it when needed. This is where an iPhone can work very well as the 'second screen'.

Recently Michael was traveling and didn't take any Mac with him; just the iPad and the iPhone. It was then he discovered that the screen of the iPhone 5 can be a great reference screen. A great second screen. As his iPhone has most of the same apps as his iPad, and all the information is synced via the cloud, it's not stored on either device. This works for editing documents (seeing one version on one device and working on a new one on the other), for taking notes while watching a YouTube video on the iPhone, for writing articles and opening the reference web sites on the iPhone... this is all very useful.

Michael sometimes even switches the iPad with the iPhone, making the iPad a second screen:

"Recently I did it the other way around. I needed to go through my recently released '10-step Productivity Course'. I simply put the iPad as my 'second screen' to play the course and I hooked up my external keyboard to the iPhone. I fired up the same Byword app on the iPhone that I use on my iPad and I took notes on my iPhone while watching the course on the iPad. More often than not I use my iPhone as my second screen or my second computer. It's actually really cool when you think about it. I have two powerful computers with me at all times and together they weigh less than 1 kg."

Augusto uses that second screen among other things as dictionary and research tool:

"I write on the iPad and edit on the iPhone, the smaller screen forces me to pay more attention and since I need to be attentive to edit, as soon as I get tired I know it is time to stop. Recently I actually started cheating in this 'second screen' thing - since I got my iPad mini, I started using my old iPad 2 as my additional screen. I can work on the iPad mini and have my iPhone or iPad 2 as a second screen. Sweet."

Two can play that game

It all sounds trivial if you think about it. 'Of course the iPhone can serve as a second screen', you'd say. Well, we knew it all along. However, only when you really make the paradigm shift and start using the iPhone as your second screen will you see lots of possibilities for making your #iPadOnly work a lot more productive.

iPhone as a recording studio

Michael is using his iPhone as his recording studio - he records the videos on it, edits and publishes them - all from the iPhone. Here's how he does it:

"Every 2-3 weeks I'm recording a short 'Productive! Show' video where I'm testing my newest productivity tips and tricks. I'm checking out what works for me and what doesn't... and I do it all via video.

Many people have asked me how I'm recording the video and which programs on my Mac I'm using to publish each episode of my Productive! Show. Well, the answer is simple: None. I'm not using any programs on the Mac. I'm recording, editing and publishing everything on the iPhone."

Let's star with the gear. Here's Michael's entire recording studio hardware-wise:

- iPhone 5
- The Glif+
- A small Hama tripod
- KV connection cable to split mic and headphone jack
- SONY ECM-AW3 wireless bluetooth microphone
- Apple Ear-pods headphones

Now let's look at the software:

- iPhone's built in camera for recording videos
- iMovie on the iPhone from Apple ($4.99 on the App Store)
- Built-in YouTube publishing capabilities of the iPhone
- Byword on the iPhone and the iPad

Here's Michael's entire flow - recording an episode of the Productive! Show from start to end.

Step 1 - prepare the iPhone:

I mount the iPhone on the tripod using the Glif and the tripod. I attach the microphone. Now, depending on the ambient noise and the sound quality I want to achieve, I'm either recording via the headphone mic or the wireless Bluetooth microphone. When using the Bluetooth microphone I'm simply attaching the KV-connection cable to the iPhone and later the Bluetooth receiver to the cable and the Bluetooth microphone to my shirt.

Step 2 - record the show:

I'm always trying to record a few short takes. Instead of recording all at once, I'll split the episode into several parts.

Step 3 - edit the show:

I dismount my entire recording studio, put the Glif, the microphone and everything else back into my bag. I sit comfortably on an armchair, attach the headphones and fire up the iMovie on the iPhone. I create a new project and start the editing process. I cut out the scenes and put them in the timeline. I add captions, define a theme and put fade-to-black at the end of the movie. Editing with the iPhone is pure fun; I do everything by finger-touching the movie. It works great. I started this workflow on the iPhone 4S, but the iPhone 5 is even better for movie editing as it's simply faster. And you can tell the difference.

Step 4 - export to camera roll

After my movie is ready, I export it to my camera roll to 720p. I don't choose full HD for now as I don't want the files to be too big. This quality is enough for a great looking video on YouTube.

Step 5 - write descriptions and other meta:

While the iPhone is generating the movie, I fire up my iPad and open Byword. I have a template set up for each video show and I follow this template to create a great title of the show, description and everything else. Once I'm done, I save the file in my iCloud folder and get back to the iPhone.

Step 6 - publish to YouTube:

I go to camera roll on the iPhone and watch my ready-to-be-published video again and see if it's the way I want it. It's never perfect but usually more than good enough. And that works for me. I click on the button 'share' and choose 'publish to YouTube'. A dialog pops up where I log in to my YouTube account and I'm being asked for video details.

This is when I switch to Byword on my iPhone and go to the iCloud section and the file with description and title I created back in Step 5 on the iPad. I copy and paste the title, description and all the other details to the YouTube upload box and upload the video.

Step 7 - bonus - add a blog post:

When the video is uploading I also copy and paste the contents of the 'description' text file to create a blog post. Once the video is uploaded I copy the embed code and publish the blog post. Then, I also submit it to the social media.

With these short 7 steps anyone can post high-quality videos on YouTube:

Voila! My entire video show has been recorded, edited and posted thanks to my iPhone (and iPad) and my entire workflow has been reduced to just 7 simple steps. None of these steps requires a Mac or any other computer. I do everything with my 'two portable computers' - the iPhone and the iPad."

www.youtube.com/iPadOnlyBook

Video #31: Creating videos on the iPhone only - iMovie on the iPhone and iPad.

The iPad and the iPhone in a family

We talked a lot about 'clouds' and 'syncing' in this book. It's great that the iPad is in sync with the clouds and through them with the iPhone... but it'd be even cooler to sync people together, right? This is why we've been testing several ways of syncing contacts and calendars with our wives in the most efficient way possible.

We are true geeks over here and we have an iPad, our wives have iPad minis and we all have iPhones. We also have two kids and complex scheduling as far as work-life balance is concerned. There are no Apple guidelines on how to create a perfect iCloud-centric family setup so after a few trial and error sessions we came up with two options and tested both of them extensively.

We've been fans of syncing calendars and contacts since the age of Nokia phones, Palm Pilots and infrared (do you remember what that was?). We remember putting our phones next to our laptops and hoping for the best. We didn't have to insert the contacts manually whenever we changed a device to a newer model. With the iPhone we had the cable sync and later a MobileMe account (yes, we both were actually paying for it). It worked great on a personal level.

However, when you're in a marriage, things get scheduled and you have more obligations. And because we work from home, our wives would assume we'd always be available. It is annoying to suddenly get a doctor's appointment scheduled in the middle of your conference call. Another problem was contacts. Texting for the information that we were supposed to have, friends, doctors, insurance information and more, were not uncommon. It had to stop.

Let's start with the basics: iCloud ID and Apple ID - how many you need and how many you can have?

Apparently you need an Apple ID (iCloud ID) for:
- iCloud storage (data, photo stream)
- Contacts, Calendar, Bookmarks and other settings
- iMessage and Facetime
- Apps and Music purchases

The thing is, you can have several Apple accounts for each of these individual things. You don't need to have one iCloud/Apple account to rule them all. You can, but you don't have to. And that's the clue to more flexibility.

Another thing is that each device (iPhone/iPad/iPod/Mac) needs to have one 'mother' account - the main iCloud account that supports its data, photo stream, backups and such. And then you can set up additional accounts for calendars, contacts, iMessage, FaceTime and purchases... if you like.

There are two ways to set up family iCloud accounts. OK, there are no 'family iCloud' accounts per se, but you can mimic them in two ways:

Version 1 - you can set up your personal iCloud account as the 'mother account' on your device and add a common iCloud account for additional syncing of contacts and calendars.

Version 2 - you can set up the same 'mother' iCloud account on all family devices and personalize them with additional iCloud accounts on each of them (for iMessage and FaceTime).

Each version has its PROs and CONs. Now, let's dive into details:

Version 1 - Personal "mother" accounts with additional central account

Michael had this setup for a few months with his wife; here's how he did it:

'I set up three iCloud accounts - one for my wife, one for me and one as a 'central' account. We used the central account as the account with our Address Book and Calendars.

On each device that belonged to my wife I set up her iCloud account as the main account and marked that this device should sync everything with the iCloud *EXCEPT* for Calendars and Contacts. I did the same for my devices.

Now, in each devices' section of 'Mail, Calendars and Contacts' I added an additional iCloud account - our 'common' iCloud account and set up the device to sync only Contacts and Calendars (and Reminders) there.

We would also set up the 'common' iCloud account for our Music and App purchases (no need to buy stuff twice, right?).

That's it. Now my wife and I could see the same calendars and contacts but have separate iCloud accounts."

Benefits of this setup: You have separate bookmarks, separate data and separate photo streams. Sounds good, right?

Disadvantages of this setup: If you sync and backup to iCloud (and we do) and are running out of free 5GB space, you need to upgrade each account separately. It's more difficult to share photos (although now it's possible through shared photo streams).

Version 2 - central "mother" account with additional personal accounts

Here's Michael's second experiment:

Here's Michael's second experiment:

"This is the other way around and this is something we later switched to and ultimately kept as our setup.

First off, we wanted to share the same iCloud account for backups now that we have an additional iPad mini backing up to the iCloud and both of our iPhones. Second thing is that we wanted to have the same photo stream. My wife said she wouldn't mind seeing an occasional screenshot of one of our apps or my other work-related stuff.

The thing is that from now on, we don't have to worry about who is taking pictures of our family - if it's me or my wife with her iPhone. The photos go to the same stream (and they are also streamed to the iPhoto on our home Mac mini).

The same applies to 'documents in the Cloud'. I'm more of an iWork guy (and I use Byword for text files) and my wife is more of an MS Office kind of girl. We don't use the same apps so there is no problem with documents overlap.

I understand with this setup we give up a little more privacy but how much privacy do you need in a marriage? We trust each other and the convenience of synced contacts, calendars and photo streams is enormous. We love it.

Apart from that I set up our personal iCloud accounts as accounts for iMessage and FaceTime. This way my wife has the same unique and personal iCloud account on her iPhone and iPad mini and MacBook Air and I have my personal iCloud account set up on all of my devices.

Recently my wife complained a little about the amount of contacts I accumulated over the years (especially business-wise) so I decided to move these to the address book on my personal iCloud account. This way our 'common' Address book is slimmer and consists of mostly people we talk to frequently."

Benefits of this setup: More integration, common photo stream and backing up all of the devices to the same iCloud account - if we need more space, we can upgrade just one 'mother' account.

Disadvantages of this setup: Less privacy as you share photo streams and documents.

That's the magic of iFamily - iCloud and iDevices in the family :-)

Version 2 was the winner for us, your milage may vary

After extensive testing and a few months of usage, in both Augusto's and Michael's family, version 2 prevailed. The benefits of having the same photos as well as not having to ask your spouse about 'that phone number' or scheduling conflicts in the calendar are great and make our lives more convenient.

CHAPTER #6
OUR IPAD GEAR

Over the last year we've been experimenting with different gear for our iPads and iPhones. When you get into choosing your gear there are really two extremes, you care for it or you don't. We are geeks and gadget-guys so we like to play with new gear, our wives don't care about it.

Part of our objective is to be mobile, and be as productive in our home-office as at the Warsaw Chopin Airport, O'Hare or Indianapolis International as at the kitchen table, or at the Starbucks seven blocks away. Because of that we have 'settled' (notice the quotation marks, 'settled' simply means in this case for now) for a few accessories for our highly mobile office that complement our #iPadOnly work.

We've divided our gadgets into three categories:

1. The essential iPad and iPhone gear - stuff we carry at all times. Things we rather have with us during the day when we're working or visiting clients and friends.

2. The rest of the iPad gear - stuff we carry when traveling - in the hotel room or in the office. These are the things we need a lot (like chargers) or might need for specific purposes.

3. The iPhone gear - stuff we need for the iPhone. We're mentioning it here as you might find it useful. Again, most of the things we carry for the iPad works with the iPhone as well.

Michael has both iPad4 and iPhone5 so he completely switched to the new Lightning port - this way both of his devices share the same cables. Augusto's big iPad continues using the old connector but his new Mini and the iPhone5 are already on the 'Lightning'. The essential iPad and iPhone gear

www.youtube.com/iPadOnlyBook

Video #32: The Essential iPad gear - and why something is important for the iPad.

The essential iPad and iPhone gear

This is the stuff we carry at all times. Things we rather have with us during the day when we're working either in our home offices or when we're on the move.

Michael's essential gear:

Logitech Ultrathin Keyboard

I've used several keyboards over the last year - the Apple's Bluetooth keyboard, ZaggKeys Flex keyboard and Logitech K750 solar keyboard.

I dismissed the Apple's keyboard right off the bat as it's just too big for me to carry around. For the first three months I used the ZaggKeys Flex keyboard and I loved it. It's very small and extremely light. However it doesn't allow me to write on my lap and it's not 'integrated' with the iPad. On the other hand I didn't want any 'folio' keyboards that would make my iPad look like a netbook. Also, I use the physical keyboard with my iPad only when I write and with my iPad in a vertical and not horizontal position.

The Ultrathin keyboard is perfect as it's more integrated with the iPad (works as a kind-of Smart Cover) and on the other hand I can detach it completely and just work with the iPad itself. This makes it great for carrying around and for typing on my lap if needed. In addition, the place to mount the iPad with the keyboard is suited for both horizontal and vertical orientation.

Side note: I also bought the Logitech K750 keyboard for my Mac mini in my home office. It has three Bluetooth buttons which help me switch between typing on my Mac, iPad and iPhone. If you have a computer at your office, this keyboard is really good.

Cosmonaut stylus

If you want to draw on the iPad, a stylus is a must. I've tried many of them, including a very well done Bamboo stylus but finally settled for the fat-boy of styluses - the Cosmonaut. It's got the great feel of a marker, forcing me to draw without resting my palms on the screen. This is the stylus I used for most of the drawings in this book.

Lightning to HDMI adapter

I use this adapter whenever I'm on the move and want to show some photos to my family or watch a video with friends. Most people I visit don't have an Apple TV (thus, no AirPlay possible) and with this adapter I just plug in to their screens using a standard HDMI cable. Works like a charm. I need to have this adapter with me at all times.

Sennheiser in-ear headphones

I carry these headphones with me and use them for listening to music on the iPhone or doing Skype or FaceTime calls on my iPhone or iPad. They fit my ear perfectly and most of all make the external environment quieter for me.

Ball point pen

Don't ask. Has nothing to do with the iPhone and the iPad. It's just super-useful to carry a ballpoint-pen with you at all times.

iPad 12W charger and Lightning cable

It's more of a 'just in case' accessory. The iPad's battery lasts the whole day, but the iPhone's doesn't. This small 12W beast charges my iPhone in no-time so I carry it around.

Augusto's essential gear:

Logitech KB110 keyboard.

"I love this keyboard, it is illuminated and the battery lasts a long time. That means that I don't need to worry about batteries or anything else. That was one of the annoyances of the Apple keyboard. Also it can use up to three devices and has an on-off switch so I don't run my battery out (that happened to me with the Apple keyboard).

InCase - Origami

This is the case designed with the Apple Keyboard in mind but nothing that a little bit of 3M double side tape can't fix. I use it with my new Logitech keyboard now.

WINGStand

This was originally a KickStarter project. I got them later from Amazon. It provides me with a great angle to type and takes up very little space in the bag. It's compatible with the iPad, the iPad Mini and the iPhone. If you use an Apple Keyboard (I don't anymore) you can even leave it attached to Keyboard.

Fisher Bullet Pen

I love these pens. They flow nicely; they write comfortably and are not that expensive. I have used them for years. They are compact but they open for a full size.

Index Cards

I always carry 2 kinds. Cheap blank ones and the Levenger

Ruled ones. There is something to be said about writing on a good paper (like Levenger).

iPhone + iPad Charger

I know the iPad will last me all day, the iPhone often doesn't. It is easier to have both all the time.

iPhone Pods extra Headset

There is nothing worse than when your headset breaks before a conference call or before you arrive someplace loud to work. I always carry a backup set.

Screen Cleaner (also Lenses Cleaner)

I wear glasses and hate it when they get too dirty, so I always have cleaner for both my glasses and the iPad and iPhone screen.

Tide Pen

It looks like a pen and contains laundry soap. It is great for cleaning your clothes on the spot.

These are the contents of my bag if I am going somewhere to work. Many times I just grab the iPad and nothing else, especially if I am not going to work for any long period of time. If I'm leaving for a longer time, I then grab my bag that it is an old Victorinox Eiffel Vertical bag.

I have been on the search to replace this bag for years, but I have not at the time of this writing found a better one, so I continue carrying it.

The rest of the iPad gear

This is the stuff we carry when traveling - in the hotel room or in the office. These are the things we need a lot (like chargers) or might need for specific purposes.

Michael's Rest of the Gear:

US adapter for Apple charger

When I'm traveling to Japan or the USA I use this small white adapter to convert my charger to a US-standard style.

iPad black leather Smart Cover

I still use the Smart Cover whenever I don't need the external keyboard. It's especially good for browsing the web and checking email. Call me boring, but my iPad is black, the external keyboard is black and my Smart Cover is black, too. 'Black' is also my favorite album by Metallica :-)

Lightning to VGA adapter

When I'm doing presentations on the iPad, I often need to connect to old projectors which don't support HDMI standard. This is where the VGA adapter comes in. With both the HDMI and VGA adapters at hand, there is hardly any projector or monitor I can't connect to. It just works.

Spare Headphones - Apple Earpods

Call me paranoid but should my main headphones get lost or break down, I carry a spare with me. For now, I carry the standard Apple Earpods that come with every iPhone.

Belkin 5-1 headphone jack splitter

It's a great small device that enables me to connect more than one headphone to my iPad or iPhone. Especially useful for watching movies with my spouse on an airplane or anywhere else when we don't want to disturb people around us with the movie we're watching.

USB Car charger

When I'm renting a car or traveling with someone else's car, this charger is a must, just in case.

Jack-to-jack audio retractable cable

I use this cable to connect to car stereo systems with my iPhone. Still many cars don't have iPod docks or Bluetooth AirPlay but they usually have audio AUX connection - using this cable I can play the music on my iPhone in the car.

Apple HDMI cable

When I'm traveling to friends, almost everyone has an HDMI cable but in hotel rooms sometimes it's very difficult to hook up to the existing HDMI cable. That's why I carry this cable with me. It's very slim and very good quality. Together with my Lightning adapter I can watch any movie in my hotel room directly from the iPad or even the iPhone.

TP-Link Nano Router + retractable LAN cable

It's the smallest router I know. I use it in hotel rooms that don't offer Wi-fi or when their Wi-fi connection is poor. I plug in the nano-router with the retractable LAN cable to the hotel's LAN network and create my own hot-spot. As both my iPhone and my iPad are already pre-configured with this router, immediately after I've connected it all of my devices appear online.

Retractable USB to micro-usb cable

I need this cable to charge micro-usb devices such as my external keyboard, the nano router, my spare Android phone and any other device that is compatible with micro USB. I actually travel with two of these cables.

Micro-usb to Lightning adapter

In order to use one of these retractable cables and be able to charge my iPhone and my iPad at the same time, I carry this adapter with me.

iPod to Lightning adapter

Most of the cars and hotel room stereos have iPod adapters and not Lightning adapters. This way I can connect to these with my iPhone and play the music directly from them.

Micro-usb to iPod adapter

I don't need it that much anymore, but in case someone needs it, I carry this adapter with me.

Bluetooth Sony microphones + KV Connection cable

When I'm recording the episodes of my Productive! Show I very often need an external microphone. For that I had to buy a KV-connection cable (which converts my iPhone jack output to a separate microphone input and headphones output). Later I plug the Sony Bluetooth wireless receiver to it and use the microphone to record videos.

Optional gear:

Seagate Media GoFlex Satelite 500GB

Recently I got this external hard drive. It works great when I need to copy movies from friends. It was especially helpful when I was reviewing my recent '10-steps to Ultimate Productivity Course'. I just had to preload everything (close to 50 GB of raw files) to the disk. The disk drive has its own battery and creates its own hot-spot so I can view the contents of the disk directly with the iPad.

Augusto's Rest of the Gear:

Bose Noise Canceling headphones

I love them. Unfortunately they are bulky; otherwise I would carry them all the time. I think they are fantastic.

Plantronics Noise Canceling headphones

This is what I use to record Podcasts, so if I am going to do just that, I bring it with me.

iPad Camera Kit for USB

It is how I connect the Plantronics to the iPad to record the podcast.

Belkin Surge Protector and 3 outlet

This little gadget is really convenient. It has a surge protector, two USB and three plugs. It has saved me in many, many places.

AirPort Express for Internet Connection

If I go to a Hotel, I always bring the AirPort Express. Cable internet in hotels is terrible, and people almost never use it, so I put my own Wi-Fi router and can quickly gain online access.

Headphone Splitter

I carry a headphone splitter in case my wife and I want to watch a movie. I may need to upgrade this soon to a splitter that can connect four so the whole family can listen to the movie if we wish.

Male to Male Headphones Cable

For Car Rentals, this is the best.

Unless I am going to do something that can only be done on the Mac, I leave the Mac behind and use LogMeIn to connect to it. If the Macbook is coming then the charger is always part of the deal.

The iPhone gear

Stuff we need for the iPhone. We're mentioning it here as you might find it useful. Again, most of the things we carry for the iPad works with the iPhone as well.

Michael's iPhone Gear:

The Glif + HAMA tiny tripod

From the makers of the Cosmonaut stylus comes the Glif - a perfect way to hook up my iPhone to a tripod and record videos and do still photos. All of the recent video shows I recorded recently for the '*Productive! Show*' have been done on the Glif.

Olloclip iPhone lenses

The iPhone takes amazing pictures but with the Olloclip iPhone lenses I can take even better ones. It's a 3-in-1 lens pack that consists of a wide-angle lens, a fish-eye (for almost 180 degree shots) and a macro lens. These are physical lenses so they also work with videos. Very useful.

Quirky Crossover

I no longer carry a wallet. All of the cards I need, my business cards and a handful of cash fit attached to the back of my iPhone with a handy pair of gummy strips. I had several wallets throughout the years but never liked any of them.. Now the iPhone with Crossover is my wallet.

Jabra SPORT bluetooth headset

I run 2-3 times a week and always take this headset with me. It came recommended from a friend and I love it. Feels great in my ears and also enables me to take calls when running (if somebody dares to interrupt my run!).

Augusto's iPhone Gear:

The Glif + Joby Mini tripod

I am working on a series of new projects and the Glif as well as the mini tripod are part of it. If I am working on that project they come with me. Other than that I keep my iPhone to the minimum.

Quirky Crossover

This is something that I recently acquired. After I saw Michael's I was convinced that I really wanted one.

This is it! This is all of our iPad and iPhone gear. The things we mentioned are really the gadgets that have helped us and served us well. This list may change in a year to come, but we try to very picky about our accessories and make sure we keep it to the minimum.

CHAPTER #7
FINAL COMMENTS

When we got the idea of writing this book we didn't know exactly what was going to be the end result. We knew we wanted to show you our #iPadOnly journey. We didn't know if this was going to be a 30 page-manifesto or an incredible book with almost 50,000 words and more than 30 videos.

This book not only gave us the opportunity to review our assumptions about our own #iPadOnly journey yet again but also made us learn new software, tips and tricks and so much more from one another.

Augusto's Final Comments

"I am grateful for this experience, I really hoped that I was able to bring you a little of my own #iPadOnly experience.

It is also Michael's fault that I spent a lot of money because of this book. He convinced me to get an iPad mini and test it and when I did, my wife took it from me and I had to get another one. OK, maybe it wasn't his fault but the inner geek in me...

Again, this has been an incredible journey. I learned so much about so many things... and I was able to discuss it almost daily with someone else; how to make my own workflows, tools and assumptions even more effective to accomplish more and be more productive in my #iPadOnly journey."

Michael's Final Comments

""I've been dying to write a book about #iPadOnly for some time now. However, in my busy schedule I knew I couldn't make it on my own. And I also wasn't sure I had enough to say to make it a book. I needed a sparing-partner for this project and I found one in Augusto.

It turns out, thanks to our synergy we had an entire book in us. As a bonus we learned so much from one another. We kept questioning each other's ideas on a regular basis... and most of all I sincerely believe we got to be part of a bigger movement where the PC's become trucks and our iPads become the mainstream computers."

www.youtube.com/iPadOnlyBook

Video #33: Final comments on our #iPadOnly book - two crazy folks writing on iPads.

Why we really wrote this book

This book's goal is not to convince you to go #iPadOnly now or tell you that you must go #iPadOnly and if you don't, you're not 'one of us'... or anything like that.

The goal is to inspire you to challenge your habits, question your workflows and take a look at how you work on your computer from a different perspective. To make you revisit your 'computer tasks' and think how you can simplify them and make them more 'fun' in the process. If we achieved that, then we consider our mission accomplished.

Reach us at ipadonly.net and let us know!

The iOS 7 wish list

www.youtube.com/iPadOnlyBook

Video #34 BONUS VIDEO: Wish list for the iPad, iOS7 and beyond.

AUGUSTO PINAUD & MICHAEL SLIWINSKI

ABOUT AUGUSTO PINAUD

Augusto Pinaud is a writer, a public speaker and a Best Selling Author in the US, UK, Germany, Spain and France. In another life, he was a lawyer in recovery and a former technology consultant and salesman. His passion is to write. He's been studying productivity and helping people get organized for the last ten years.

Augusto lives in Fort Wayne, Indiana. He is married and has a little girl, a boy and two dogs that keep him company. He spends his day teaching his daughter and son various things, writing and washing dishes, because he believes in what Agatha Christie once said: "The best time for planning a book is while you're doing the dishes."

My blog: www.augustopinaud.com
Twitter: apinaud
Email: augusto@augustopinaud.com
Facebook: http://www.facebook.com/augustopinaud/

OTHER BOOKS BY AUGUSTO PINAUD

Productivity (English):
- *25 Tips for Productivity*
- *No*
- *4:00 AM A Productivity Argument*

Fiction (English):
- *The Writer*
- *Putsch. A Hannah Fisher Thriller*

Productivity (Spanish):
- *25 Consejos de Productividad*
- *No*
- *4:00 A.M. Un Argumento de Productividad*

ABOUT MICHAEL SLIWINSKI

Michael Sliwinski is a productivity guy - he's mostly known as the founder of Nozbe.com - a time and project management web application with native apps for the Mac, Windows, iPhone, iPad and Android.

Michael is also the editor of the Productive! Magazine - a digital magazine featuring articles and interviews with the smartest productivity gurus in the world. He's also recording productivity videos (Productive! Show) and posts them along with his other articles on his personal web site. Michael also writes regular columns for a various magazines and speaks publicly on productivity and startup businesses.

He lives in Europe with his wife and two daughters.

Michael's blog: www.michaelsliwinski.com
Twitter: MSliwinski
Email: michael@sliwinski.com
Facebook: http://www.facebook.com/MichaelSliwinski.Com/

AUGUSTO PINAUD & MICHAEL SLIWINSKI

THANKS BY AUGUSTO PINAUD

To my wife, daughter and son, who are simply amazing. I will never get tired of saying that.

To Michael Sliwinski, a friend and amazing co-author of this book. This had been an honor for me, as well as a learning opportunity.

To Tara Rodden Robinson, my friend, an unconditional supporter, and teacher.

To Kenn Rudolph, not only my friend but who also created the incredible covers of my other books and was willing to teach my sister for this one.

To those who always believed in me and who now smile when learning that I am a writer.

To those kind and generous eyes that read this when it looked like a minefield, full of spelling and grammar errors.

To my parents, friends and family.

To Lori who kindly reviewed this book before it was ready for primetime and leave their comment for us to use.

To Omar Carreño Robles y José Maria Villarmeal who share with me their journey to get more from their iPad and get closer to #iPadOnly

To all those who took the time to read this or any of my books.

To those who had given their reviews on this book or any other of my books.

To those people who in some way or another have helped me make this a reality.

THANKS BY MICHAEL SLIWINSKI

To my family - my three amazing girls: my wife Ewelina and my daughters Milena and Emilia. Can't imagine my life without them.

To Augusto for accepting to be my co-author on a whim and later for his patience and great support. For being an ideal sparing-partner who kept questioning everything we both were doing. And for being a great friend. The best friend I never met in person yet, actually :-)

To Lori - our Productive! Magazine editor - for her constant support and for doing an amazing job editing this book. You're the best.

To Radek - Nozbe's chief designer - for bearing with us as we couldn't decide on the book's cover and for helping us out with the web site.

To Tomasz - Nozbe's CTO - for helping us out with this project and most of all, for managing Nozbe's team when I had to switch off and write this book. I can't thank you enough, man.

To Delfina - Nozbe's chief of customer support - for keeping our Nozbe customers happy when I had to be offline to write.

To Dominik - the chief editor of iMagazine - for letting me write for his magazine and for supporting me in my #iPadOnly journey and helping me with his vast Apple knowledge.

To other people I drew the #iPadOnly inspiration from: Jakub Krzych, Simon Grabowski, … and many more.

And to our late Steve Jobs and Apple, for manufacturing this amazing device that totally changed the way I work on the computer. For making our work more fun and touchy-feely :-))